# Contents

# Acknowledgements

**This survey could not have taken place without the cooperation of the children, their parents, teachers and headteachers in the participating schools. We are very grateful for their help.**

The authors would like to thank the following colleagues at the NFER for their invaluable work during the PIRLS survey and in the production of this report:

> Maria Charles and colleagues in Research Data Services who undertook all the contact with the sampled schools
>
> Joan Howell and the printing team who organised the reproduction of the test instruments and questionnaires
>
> Alissa Cooper who helped to coordinate the marking
>
> John Hanson and colleagues in the Database Production Group who organised all the data capture and cleaning
>
> Ian Schagen and fellow statisticians in the Statistics Research and Analysis Group who undertook additional statistical analyses
>
> Stuart Gordon for the design of the cover
>
> Mary Hargreaves who prepared the text for publication
>
> Alison Lawson for overseeing production and publication.

PIRLS is a collaborative project with a number of international partners. We would like to thank:

> the staff of Statistics Canada for their help and expertise in sampling issues
>
> staff at the IEA Data Processing Center in Hamburg for their work in preparing the data files
>
> the staff of the International Study Center at Boston College and the IEA Directorate in Amsterdam for their support throughout the PIRLS project.

PIRLS in England was commissioned by the Department for Education and Skills. We would like to acknowledge the support and guidance of the steering committee at the DfES.

# Executive Summary

## 1. Background to the study

1.1 The Progress in International Reading Literacy Study is a comparative study of the reading achievement of ten-year-olds in 2001. It is conducted under the auspices of the International Association for the Evaluation of Educational Achievement. Similar surveys will be carried out every five years in order to measure trends.

1.2 Over 140,000 pupils in 35 countries participated in PIRLS 2001.

1.3 The tests and questionnaires used in the study were developed by an international consortium and approved by all participating countries.

1.4 There were stringent criteria for participating countries to meet in order to ensure the results were comparable from country to country.

1.5 The survey in England was conducted by the National Foundation for Educational Research (NFER) and involved 3156 children in year 5.

## 2. Reading achievement

2.1 Children in England are, on average, among the most able readers in the world at about the age of ten. England was ranked third in terms of reading achievement of those countries involved, with only Sweden and The Netherlands higher.

2.2 Pupils in England scored more highly than those in the major European countries of France, Germany and Italy. They also scored significantly more highly than the other English-speaking countries in the survey: United States, New Zealand and Scotland.

2.3 In England, performance in reading for literary purposes (stories) was significantly better than performance in reading information passages. A similar difference was found in most English-speaking countries. In contrast, many continental European countries had higher scores for informational reading.

2.4 England is one of the countries with the widest span of attainment. Its most able pupils are the highest scoring in the survey, but its low achieving pupils are ranked much lower. This pattern is a consistent one in English-speaking countries, but continental European countries are more likely to have a similar standing for their high and low achieving children, leading to a narrower range of attainment.

2.5 In a similar study undertaken in the 1990s by the NFER, England had a performance around the international average, rather than the high position achieved in 2001 (Brooks *et al*, 1996).

2.6 Students in England also achieved a high position in the PISA study of reading literacy of 15-year-olds undertaken in 2000. However, there is little correlation between performance in the two surveys of the countries which took part in both, perhaps illustrating the volatility of educational systems in an age of reform.

## 3. Gender differences in reading achievement

3.1 Girls performed better than boys in all participating countries in PIRLS. In England, girls did particularly well on the literary texts.

3.2 The difference between the scores of boys and girls in England is smaller for the better readers, compared to the difference between boys and girls in the weakest group.

3.3 Girls do better than boys in the national tests in England at the end of key stages 1 and 2 (ages 7 and 11). Girls also scored more highly in the PISA study of the reading skills of 15-year-olds in 2000.

## 4. The PIRLS reading literacy tests

4.1 PIRLS adopts this definition of reading literacy:

*The ability to understand and use those written language forms required by society and/or valued by the individual. Young readers can construct meaning from a variety of texts. They read to learn, to participate in communities of readers, and for enjoyment.*

4.2 The assessment includes different types of reading passage. Half of them are stories, and the other half give factual information.

4.3 The top ten per cent of children showed a complete understanding of what they had read, bringing together ideas and forming opinions based on the text. Those in the lowest band of performance could select the right answer to a simple question.

4.4 Children in England following the National Curriculum were well prepared for the demands of the PIRLS test. The National Curriculum, too, requires both literature and factual reading. Children are taught to use inference, to formulate opinions and to analyse what they have read.

4.5 The children in PIRLS went on to take their national key stage 2 tests a year later, in 2002 and the results on the assessments were consistent. Some of the questions in the key stage 2 test are similar to those in PIRLS and a few are more demanding than anything in PIRLS.

## 5. Reading at home

5.1 The parents who responded to the questionnaire in England tended to be those with higher achieving children. Their homes have, on average, a very high level of educational resources. The parents have a very positive attitude to reading and expose their children to a high level of literacy activity before they start school (for example, reading stories, playing word games), which declines as the children get older.

5.2 Despite a higher score on the international reading assessment, ten-year-old pupils in England have a poorer attitude towards reading, and read less often for fun than pupils of the same age in other countries. Boys have a less positive attitude to reading than girls.

5.3 Ten-year-old children in England tend to play computer games more frequently than their international peers, watch television more frequently and for longer. The relationship between these activities and reading achievement is a complex one and requires further study.

# 6. The teachers and the schools involved in PIRLS

6.1 Children in England start school earlier, show more reading readiness and have a higher level of early learning skills than their international peers. They are taught for more hours, in larger classes and by teachers who are more highly qualified. England is amongst the countries with the highest numbers of books in schools and the best access to specialist staff for the teaching of reading.

6.2 More pupils in England are taught using a variety of grouping arrangements than elsewhere and children of different reading abilities are more likely to use different materials. Children in England were more likely than those in any other country in PIRLS to be taught by teachers who use a variety of children's books in their teaching of reading.

6.3 Teachers found the resource materials and training provided for the national literacy strategy (NLS) useful. Guided reading sessions were frequently used by teachers in the survey, who recorded broad agreement about the activities within these sessions. Teachers believe that the NLS has introduced pupils to a wider range of texts.

6.4 Ten-year-old pupils in England are likely to have less reading homework and their parents to have less formal involvement with the schools than the international average.

6.5 The range of reading ability in rural and urban schools, and in schools with the highest and lowest proportions of economically disadvantaged pupils, is wider than in most other countries.

6.6 Children in England are amongst those with the greatest access to computers and to the Internet of any in the survey.

# 7. Influence of background factors on reading achievement

7.1 When all other factors are controlled, girls scored more highly than boys in the PIRLS assessments in England. Older pupils tended to score more highly, as did pupils born in the UK. Children with more books in the home, those who are more positive about reading and the more confident readers tended to have higher scores, whereas those from larger families and those who reported doing more reading activities at home and at school, tended to have lower scores.

7.2 Girls, children born in the UK and those from smaller families, tended to be more positive and confident about reading.

7.3 Girls, children in schools where the headteacher reported higher levels of disadvantage, and children who were born outside the UK, tended to be involved in more reading activities at home and at school.

7.4 Boys tended to report higher levels of television viewing than girls, as did children born in the UK and those from smaller families.

7.5 Children with more books at home tended to be higher achieving, to be more positive and confident about reading, to participate in reading activities at home more frequently, to talk more about their reading and to make more use of computers.

# 1. Background to PIRLS 2001

**The Progress in International Reading Literacy Study is a comparative study of reading achievement of ten-year-olds in 2001. It is conducted under the auspices of the International Association for the Evaluation of Educational Achievement. Similar surveys will be carried out every five years in order to measure trends.**

- Over 140,000 pupils in 35 countries participated in PIRLS 2001.

- The tests and questionnaires used in the study were developed by an international consortium and approved by all participating countries.

- There were stringent criteria for participating countries to meet in order to ensure the results were comparable from country to country.

- The survey in England was conducted by the National Foundation for Educational Research (NFER) and involved 3156 children in year 5.

## 1.1 Introduction

### Objectives of the study

'Reading literacy is one of the most important abilities students acquire as they progress through their early school years. It is the foundation for learning across all subjects, it can be used for recreation and for personal growth, and it equips young children with the ability to participate fully in their communities and the larger society.'

(Campbell *et al*, 2001)

The Progress in International Reading Literacy Study 2001 was conducted by the International Association for the Evaluation of Educational Achievement (IEA). The study is an investigation of children's reading literacy and the factors associated with its acquisition in 35 countries around the world. The first assessment took place in 2001 and future assessments are planned on a five-yearly cycle, with the objective of monitoring trends in reading attainment.

## Countries participating in PIRLS 2001

| | | | |
|---|---|---|---|
| Argentina | Germany | Latvia | Russian Federation |
| Belize | Greece | Lithuania | Scotland |
| Bulgaria | Hong Kong, SAR | Macedonia, Rep. of | Singapore |
| Canada (Ontario/Quebec) | Hungary | Moldova, Rep. of | Slovak Republic |
| Colombia | Iceland | Morocco | Slovenia |
| Cyprus | Iran, Islamic Rep. of | The Netherlands | Sweden |
| Czech Republic | Israel | New Zealand | Turkey |
| England | Italy | Norway | United States |
| France | Kuwait | Romania | |

## Roles of consortium members

The International Study Center at Boston College, Boston, United States, was responsible for the overall design, development and implementation of PIRLS. This included establishing the procedures, overseeing instrument development, conducting training and carrying out quality assurance measures. An international report of the results of PIRLS 2001 has been produced by the ISC (Mullis *et al*, 2003).

The IEA Data Processing Center (DPC) in Hamburg, Germany was responsible for processing and verifying the data from all of the countries, and constructing the international database.

The Special Surveys Methods Group of Statistics Canada in Ottawa, Canada, was responsible for all sampling activities in PIRLS, including developing the sampling procedures and documentation, and assisting participants in adapting the PIRLS sampling design to local conditions. The independent sampling referee was from Westat in the United States.

The National Foundation for Educational Research in England and Wales (NFER) in Slough, England, had major responsibility for developing the PIRLS reading literacy tests, including collecting reading passages from the participating countries and developing items and mark schemes.

The Educational Testing Service (ETS) in Princeton, New Jersey, United States, contributed significantly to the development of the PIRLS framework and the reading assessment. ETS also provided software and support for scaling the PIRLS achievement results.

The PIRLS instruments – tests and questionnaires – were developed over a two-year period, from 1999 to 2001. At each stage of development, all the participating countries reviewed the emerging materials and revisions were made in the light of any concerns that emerged. In autumn 2000, there was a field trial in 30 countries which allowed final refinement of the instruments.

## PIRLS in England

The Department for Education and Skills commissioned the National Foundation for Educational Research to carry out PIRLS in England. The NFER undertook all contact with sampled schools, the adaptation of the instruments and manuals for use in England, the training of test administrators, the marking of the survey instruments and the data capture. Additional analyses included in this report were conducted by the NFER.

## 1.2    Conduct of the survey

In order to establish and maintain comparability between all the participating countries, PIRLS was conducted according to a rigorous set of procedures (Gonzalez *et al*, 2002). These specified:

- participation of a representative sample of pupils using a two-stage sampling design with probability-proportional-to-size sampling

- minimum response rates before the inclusion of replacement schools

- at least 95 per cent coverage of the target population

- comparability in instruments and questionnaires by having all translations and adaptations independently verified

- consistent implementation of the survey procedures according to the internationally-agreed standards, including random quality control visits to schools by national observers and international monitors

- multiple-marking exercises to assess scoring reliability

- rigorous data-cleaning procedures, nationally and at the Data Processing Center.

### Target population

The target population for PIRLS was defined as:

> *All students enrolled in the upper of the two adjacent grades that contain the largest proportion of 9-year-olds at the time of testing.*

This age group was targeted because at this point in children's development they have learned to read and are now starting to read to learn.  It is also the age of pupils assessed in the IEA TIMSS (Trends in International Mathematics and Science Study).

For most of the participating countries, this is the fourth grade.  In England, this is year 5, due to an earlier entry into compulsory schooling.  This is also the case for New Zealand and Scotland.  The average age of pupils participating in the study was 10.3 years.  The average age of pupils in England was 10.2 years.  The pupils with the lowest average age were those in Cyprus and in Iceland (9.7 years) and the pupils in Morocco were on average the oldest with a mean age of 11.2 years.

The nationally defined population was the sampling frame from which the first stage of sampling took place.  In England, as in most other countries, special schools and very small schools were excluded from the nationally defined population.

### Within-school exclusions

Each country had to define its own within-school exclusions.  These were limited to pupils for whom the PIRLS tests were inappropriate and the definition adopted in each country had to be approved by the International Study Center at Boston College and by Statistics Canada. The definitions of within-school exclusions applied in England are included in Appendix 1.

### Response rates

Response rates are detailed in Appendix 1.  This includes the response rates of the main sample and the use of replacement schools; the coverage of the nationally desired population and the achieved response rates to each of the four questionnaires.

The response rate from sampled schools to invitations to participate in PIRLS 2001 was lower in England than in all other countries with the exception of The Netherlands and Lithuania. This apparent reluctance to participate in international studies is not a new phenomenon. It may be due to the autonomy of schools in England, in contrast to the situation in many other countries. There are also many other national and local initiatives in England which request the involvement of schools. A quarter of schools which declined to participate cited these other requests as a reason for refusal.

England met the sampling requirements with the inclusion of replacement schools. The achieved coverage of the nationally defined population in England was 94 per cent whereas the international target was 95 per cent. For this reason, data from England is footnoted.

An additional check on the representativeness of the achieved sample was undertaken for England. The results of the key stage 2 reading tests in 2002 were collected for the pupils participating in PIRLS. These tests were taken exactly one year later and results were available for 84 per cent of the PIRLS sample. These results were compared with the national distribution of key stage 2 reading levels for 2002 (recalculated to exclude pupils who were absent or disapplied from the tests). The results of this comparison are shown in Table 1.1.

**Table 1.1   Reading level achieved by PIRLS sample in key stage 2 reading test in 2002 compared to national distribution**

| Level | English | | Reading | | Writing | |
|---|---|---|---|---|---|---|
| | PIRLS | National | PIRLS | National | PIRLS | National |
| Below 3 | 4% | 6% | 5% | 7% | 5% | 7% |
| Level 3 | 16% | 18% | 11% | 12% | 31% | 32% |
| Level 4 | 50% | 47% | 44% | 43% | 45% | 44% |
| Level 5 | 30% | 29% | 40% | 39% | 19% | 17% |

Recalculated from DfES data sets (see *Autumn Package 2002 Key Stage 2 National Summary Results*).

Table 1.1 shows a very good match between the national population and the PIRLS sample, with a slight under-representation of children working at the lower levels. Although the difference between the distributions was statistically significant, the differences in the distributions were slight. The correlation between pupils' scores on PIRLS and on the key stage 2 reading test one year later was high at 0.77.

Very high response rates (over 94 per cent) were achieved for the three questionnaires completed by pupils, teachers and headteachers in the participating schools. The response rate to the home questionnaire was considerably lower at 55 per cent. It does appear that this resulted in an unrepresentative sample of pupils for whom data about literacy experiences in the home is available, with an over-representation of the higher achieving pupils. The potential unrepresentativeness of the home questionnaire data needs to be considered when information derived from this source is reviewed. These tables are footnoted in this report.

Additional information about the representativeness of the sampled and participating schools in England on pupil and school level variables is contained in Appendix 1.

## Survey procedures

The survey was conducted between 14–23 May 2001. Once schools had agreed to participate and had nominated a contact person, the test administration date was finalised.

Test administrators were appointed and trained by the NFER and followed the procedure as detailed in the Test Administrator Manual. This was adapted for use in England from the manual produced by the International Study Center.

The questionnaires due to be completed by the headteacher and the class teacher were sent in advance to the school contacts. These were then collected on the day of testing by the test administrator and returned to the NFER with the test materials.

The survey required two timetabled sessions in schools, both on the same day. The first was for the administration of the reading tests and the second was for the completion of the pupil questionnaires. Materials were kept secure and test administrators took the booklets into schools and returned them to the NFER.

Test administrators gave the home questionnaires to the school contact for distribution to the participating pupils. The questionnaires were labelled with unique identifiers. The completed home questionnaires were returned directly to the NFER using reply-paid labels.

The marking of the constructed response questions in the tests was carried out by markers trained by NFER staff who had attended the international marker training conference.

## Assessment design

In order to ensure that the assessment material provided valid and reliable measures of reading literacy and yet were manageable for 9–10-year-olds, a matrix sampling technique was used. This enabled all assessment instruments to be linked so that ultimately performance of all pupils could be placed on a single scale using Item Response Theory (IRT) methods, but meant that each participating pupil took just a part of the whole assessment.

The material was divided into assessment 'blocks'. Each block consisted of a passage of between 400 and 700 words and its associated items. There were four blocks containing literary texts and four containing information texts. Detail about the passages and the items is contained in Chapter 4. The blocks were combined into test booklets with two blocks in one booklet. One booklet was a colour 'reader'; this was a separate stimulus booklet containing two reading passages and with the test items in an accompanying response booklet. Pupils were given up to 40 minutes for the completion of each assessment block.

**Table 1.2   Distribution of assessment blocks between booklets**

| | Booklet 1 | Booklet 2 | Booklet 3 | Booklet 4 | Booklet 5 | Booklet 6 | Booklet 7 | Booklet 8 | Booklet 9 | Booklet 10 (reader) |
|---|---|---|---|---|---|---|---|---|---|---|
| **Assessment blocks** | Lit 1 | Lit 2 | Lit 3 | Inf 1 | Inf 2 | Inf 3 | Lit 1 | Inf 2 | Inf 3 | Lit 4 |
| | Lit 2 | Lit 3 | Inf 1 | Inf 2 | Inf 3 | Lit 1 | Inf 1 | Lit 2 | Lit 3 | Inf 4 |

All participating pupils were randomly allocated an assessment booklet and all materials had unique identifiers.

## Quality control

### Monitoring visits

In order to monitor the quality of the data-collection exercise, two forms of monitoring were introduced. International quality control monitors observed the test administration in a random selection of 15 schools. These monitors were trained by the International Study Center. In addition, national observers, trained by the national centre, observed test administration in a further 10 per cent of schools, randomly selected. The international and national monitors provided comprehensive reports on their visits to the ISC and the national centre respectively.

### Reliability marking

In order to establish marking reliability, a random sample of 200 responses to each of the constructed response items was independently marked by two markers. The percentage agreement between the two markers provides a measure of the reliability of the marking process. The first marker marked on sheets rather than in the pupil booklets and the second marker recorded decisions in the booklets, as for the rest of the marking. The agreement was 96 per cent on constructed response items in England, with a range of exact agreement from 81 per cent to 100 per cent.

nfer

# 2. Children's Achievement in Reading

This chapter summarises reading achievement for each of the countries that took part in PIRLS 2001. The discussion and some comparisons focus on countries of particular interest as comparators to England – developed countries in the OECD, English-speaking countries, Western European countries and states seeking accession to the European Union. Some comparisons are made with the data from the Programme for International Student Assessment (PISA) study, which assessed 15-year-olds in 2000.

- Children in England are, on average, among the most able readers in the world at about the age of ten. England was ranked third in terms of Reading Achievement with only Sweden and The Netherlands higher.

- Pupils in England scored more highly than those in the major European countries of France, Germany and Italy. They also scored significantly more highly than the other English-speaking countries in the survey: United States, New Zealand and Scotland.

- In England, performance in reading for literary purposes was significantly better than performance in reading for information. A similar difference was found in most English-speaking countries. In contrast, many continental European countries had higher scores for informational reading.

- England is one of the countries with the widest span of attainment. Its most able pupils are the highest scoring in the survey, but its low achieving pupils are ranked much lower. This pattern is a consistent one in English-speaking countries, but continental European countries are more likely to have a similar standing for their high and low achieving children, leading to a narrower range of attainment.

- In a similar study undertaken in the 1990s by the NFER, England had a performance around the international average, rather than the high position achieved in 2001 (Brooks *et al*, 1996).

- Students in England also achieved a high position in the PISA study of reading literacy of 15-year-olds undertaken in 2000. However, there is little correlation between performance in the two surveys, perhaps illustrating the volatility of educational systems in an age of reform.

## 2.1 Reading achievement

Figure 2.1 presents the distribution of student achievement in reading for the 35 countries that participated in PIRLS 2001. The countries are shown in order of average (mean) scale score. The scores range from 561 for Sweden down to 327 for Belize. The international average is 500. PIRLS 2001 used Item Response Theory (IRT) to summarise the results on a scale with a mean of 500 and a standard deviation of 100. Pupils' responses have been summarised on a common metric even though individual children responded for different items in the reading test. Further details are given within Appendix A of the International Report in the section titled '*IRT Scaling and Data Analysis*' (Mullis *et al*, 2003).

Figure 2.1 also indicates whether a country's scale score is significantly above or below the international average. Twenty-three countries were significantly above the international average and ten significantly below this average. Many of those above average were European countries, or those with developed economies. Those below the international average were largely outside Europe and with developing economies.

England was ranked third in terms of the Reading Achievement scale score, with Sweden and The Netherlands higher. Other English-testing countries (who took substantially the same test) were above the international average but with lower scores than England: United States, New Zealand, Scotland and Singapore. Canada (Ontario), testing largely in English, was also well above the international average. Scores for the major European countries (Germany, Italy and France) were above the international average but below those for England.

The European states seeking accession to the European Union were spread across the range of achievement, with Bulgaria having similar performance to England, and the Baltic states of Latvia and Lithuania also having high average scores. Hungary and the Czech Republic were among the top third of countries but the Slovak Republic, Romania, Slovenia and Cyprus were all close to the international average.

PIRLS 2001 devoted considerable effort to maximising comparability across the ages and grades tested. However, because education systems are so different, there are many school starting ages, leading to different lengths of schooling. Most countries tested children after four years of formal schooling[1] but for England, New Zealand and Scotland pupils were tested after five years of schooling. Nevertheless, the average age of the children tested in England was 10.2 years, virtually the same as the international average (10.3 years).

Figure 2.1 also indicates information about the range of scores in each country and the confidence interval for the main score. The dark boxes in the centre of each country's bar show the 95 per cent confidence interval around the average achievement of each country. The start and end of the bars show the 5th and 95th percentiles for pupil achievement in each country. Hence the length of the bar indicates the range of achievement in that country. The 25th and 75th percentiles are also shown. Each percentile point indicates the percentage of children performing below and above that point on the scale. For example, 25 per cent of pupils in each country performed below the 25th percentile of that country and 75 per cent performed above it. The range between the 25th and 75th represents performance by the middle half of the pupils. In most countries, the range of performance for the middle group was around 100 scale points.

---

[1]   The length of formal schooling has been determined by the International Study Center from the information provided by each country. It does not correspond exactly to years of compulsory schooling (Mullis *et al*, 2002).

## Figure 2.1 Distribution of reading achievement

| Countries | Reading Achievement Scale Score | | Average Scale Score | Years of Formal Schooling | Average Age |
|---|---|---|---|---|---|
| Sweden | | ▲ | 561 (2.2) | 4 | 10.8 |
| † Netherlands | | ▲ | 554 (2.5) | 4 | 10.3 |
| †2a England | | ▲ | 553 (3.4) | 5 | 10.2 |
| Bulgaria | | ▲ | 550 (3.8) | 4 | 10.9 |
| Latvia | | ▲ | 545 (2.3) | 4 | 11.0 |
| * 1 Canada (O,Q) | | ▲ | 544 (2.4) | 4 | 10.0 |
| 1 Lithuania | | ▲ | 543 (2.6) | 4 | 10.9 |
| Hungary | | ▲ | 543 (2.2) | 4 | 10.7 |
| † United States | | ▲ | 542 (3.8) | 4 | 10.2 |
| Italy | | ▲ | 541 (2.4) | 4 | 9.8 |
| Germany | | ▲ | 539 (1.9) | 4 | 10.5 |
| Czech Republic | | ▲ | 537 (2.3) | 4 | 10.5 |
| New Zealand | | ▲ | 529 (3.6) | 5 | 10.1 |
| † Scotland | | ▲ | 528 (3.6) | 5 | 9.8 |
| Singapore | | ▲ | 528 (5.2) | 4 | 10.1 |
| 2a Russian Federation | | ▲ | 528 (4.4) | 3 or 4 | 10.3 |
| Hong Kong, SAR | | ▲ | 528 (3.1) | 4 | 10.2 |
| France | | ▲ | 525 (2.4) | 4 | 10.1 |
| 2a Greece | | ▲ | 524 (3.5) | 4 | 9.9 |
| Slovak Republic | | ▲ | 518 (2.8) | 4 | 10.3 |
| Iceland | | ▲ | 512 (1.2) | 4 | 9.7 |
| Romania | | ▲ | 512 (4.6) | 4 | 11.1 |
| 2b Israel | | ▲ | 509 (2.8) | 4 | 10.0 |
| Slovenia | | | 502 (2.0) | 3 | 9.8 |
| International Avg. | | | 500 (0.6) | 4 | 10.3 |
| Norway | | | 499 (2.9) | 4 | 10.0 |
| Cyprus | | ▼ | 494 (3.0) | 4 | 9.7 |
| Moldova, Rep. of | | ▼ | 492 (4.0) | 4 | 10.8 |
| Turkey | | ▼ | 449 (3.5) | 4 | 10.2 |
| Macedonia, Rep. of | | ▼ | 442 (4.6) | 4 | 10.7 |
| Colombia | | ▼ | 422 (4.4) | 4 | 10.5 |
| Argentina | | ▼ | 420 (5.9) | 4 | 10.2 |
| Iran, Islamic Rep. of | | ▼ | 414 (4.2) | 4 | 10.4 |
| Kuwait | | ▼ | 396 (4.3) | 4 | 9.9 |
| ‡ Morocco | | ▼ | 350 (9.6) | 4 | 11.2 |
| Belize | | ▼ | 327 (4.7) | 4 | 9.8 |
| | | | | | |
| * Ontario (Canada) | | ▲ | 548 (3.3) | 4 | 9.9 |
| * Quebec (Canada) | | ▲ | 537 (3.0) | 4 | 10.2 |

200   300   400   500   600   700   800

Percentiles of Performance

5th   25th   75th   95th

Average and 95% Confidence Interval (±2SE)

▲ Country average significantly higher than international average

▼ Country average significantly lower than international average

* Canada is represented by the provinces of Ontario and Quebec only. The international average does not include the results from these provinces separately.
† Met guidelines for sample participation rates only after replacement schools were included.
‡ Nearly satisfying guidelines for sample participation rates after replacement schools were included.
1 National Desired Population does not cover all of International Desired Population. Because coverage falls below 65%, Canada is annotated Canada (O, Q) for the provinces of Ontario and Quebec only.
2a National Defined Population covers less than 95% of National Desired Population.
2b National Defined Population covers less than 80% of National Desired Population.
( ) Standard errors appear in parentheses. Because results are rounded to the nearest whole number, some totals may appear inconsistent.

Source: IEA Progress in International Reading Literacy Study (PIRLS) 2001

The figure illustrates that England is one of the countries with a wide span of pupil attainment, and this aspect of the results is discussed further below.

PIRLS 2001 found substantial differences in performance across the range of countries. However, as Figure 2.1 indicates, when the confidence intervals are considered, there was very little difference in performance between any country and the next higher or next lower performing country. Figure 2.2 shows whether or not the differences in average achievement between pairs of countries are statistically significant. To use this figure, select a country of interest, and read across the table. A chevron pointing upwards indicates significantly higher performance than the comparison country listed across the top. A chevron pointing down

**Figure 2.2   Multiple comparisons of average reading achievement**

Instructions: Read across the row for a country to compare performance with the countries listed along the top of the chart. The symbols indicate whether the average achievement of the country in the row is significantly lower than that of the comparison country, significantly higher than that of the comparison country, or if there is no statistically significant differences between the average achievement of the two countries.

| | Sweden | Netherlands | England | Bulgaria | Latvia | Canada (O,Q) | Lithuania | Hungary | United States | Italy | Germany | Czech Republic | New Zealand | Scotland | Singapore | Russian Federation | Hong Kong, SAR | France | Greece | Slovak Republic | Iceland | Romania | Israel | Slovenia | Norway | Cyprus | Moldova, Rep. of | Turkey | Macedonia, Rep. of | Colombia | Argentina | Iran, Islamic Rep. of | Kuwait | Morocco | Belize |
|---|---|---|---|---|---|---|---|---|---|---|---|---|---|---|---|---|---|---|---|---|---|---|---|---|---|---|---|---|---|---|---|---|---|---|---|
| Sweden | | ▲ | ▲ | ▲ | ▲ | ▲ | ▲ | ▲ | ▲ | ▲ | ▲ | ▲ | ▲ | ▲ | ▲ | ▲ | ▲ | ▲ | ▲ | ▲ | ▲ | ▲ | ▲ | ▲ | ▲ | ▲ | ▲ | ▲ | ▲ | ▲ | ▲ | ▲ | ▲ | ▲ | ▲ |
| Netherlands | ▼ | | | ▲ | ▲ | ▲ | ▲ | ▲ | ▲ | ▲ | ▲ | ▲ | ▲ | ▲ | ▲ | ▲ | ▲ | ▲ | ▲ | ▲ | ▲ | ▲ | ▲ | ▲ | ▲ | ▲ | ▲ | ▲ | ▲ | ▲ | ▲ | ▲ | ▲ | ▲ | ▲ |
| England | ▼ | | | | ▲ | ▲ | ▲ | ▲ | ▲ | ▲ | ▲ | ▲ | ▲ | ▲ | ▲ | ▲ | ▲ | ▲ | ▲ | ▲ | ▲ | ▲ | ▲ | ▲ | ▲ | ▲ | ▲ | ▲ | ▲ | ▲ | ▲ | ▲ | ▲ | ▲ | ▲ |
| Bulgaria | ▼ | ▼ | | | | ▲ | ▲ | ▲ | ▲ | ▲ | ▲ | ▲ | ▲ | ▲ | ▲ | ▲ | ▲ | ▲ | ▲ | ▲ | ▲ | ▲ | ▲ | ▲ | ▲ | ▲ | ▲ | ▲ | ▲ | ▲ | ▲ | ▲ | ▲ | ▲ | ▲ |
| Latvia | ▼ | ▼ | ▼ | | | | | | | | | ▲ | ▲ | ▲ | ▲ | ▲ | ▲ | ▲ | ▲ | ▲ | ▲ | ▲ | ▲ | ▲ | ▲ | ▲ | ▲ | ▲ | ▲ | ▲ | ▲ | ▲ | ▲ | ▲ | ▲ |
| Canada (O,Q) | ▼ | ▼ | ▼ | ▼ | | | | | | | | | ▲ | ▲ | ▲ | ▲ | ▲ | ▲ | ▲ | ▲ | ▲ | ▲ | ▲ | ▲ | ▲ | ▲ | ▲ | ▲ | ▲ | ▲ | ▲ | ▲ | ▲ | ▲ | ▲ |
| Lithuania | ▼ | ▼ | ▼ | ▼ | | | | | | | | | ▲ | ▲ | ▲ | ▲ | ▲ | ▲ | ▲ | ▲ | ▲ | ▲ | ▲ | ▲ | ▲ | ▲ | ▲ | ▲ | ▲ | ▲ | ▲ | ▲ | ▲ | ▲ | ▲ |
| Hungary | ▼ | ▼ | ▼ | ▼ | | | | | | | | | ▲ | ▲ | ▲ | ▲ | ▲ | ▲ | ▲ | ▲ | ▲ | ▲ | ▲ | ▲ | ▲ | ▲ | ▲ | ▲ | ▲ | ▲ | ▲ | ▲ | ▲ | ▲ | ▲ |
| United States | ▼ | ▼ | ▼ | ▼ | | | | | | | | | ▲ | ▲ | ▲ | ▲ | ▲ | ▲ | ▲ | ▲ | ▲ | ▲ | ▲ | ▲ | ▲ | ▲ | ▲ | ▲ | ▲ | ▲ | ▲ | ▲ | ▲ | ▲ | ▲ |
| Italy | ▼ | ▼ | ▼ | ▼ | | | | | | | | | ▲ | ▲ | ▲ | ▲ | ▲ | ▲ | ▲ | ▲ | ▲ | ▲ | ▲ | ▲ | ▲ | ▲ | ▲ | ▲ | ▲ | ▲ | ▲ | ▲ | ▲ | ▲ | ▲ |
| Germany | ▼ | ▼ | ▼ | ▼ | | | | | | | | | ▲ | ▲ | ▲ | ▲ | ▲ | ▲ | ▲ | ▲ | ▲ | ▲ | ▲ | ▲ | ▲ | ▲ | ▲ | ▲ | ▲ | ▲ | ▲ | ▲ | ▲ | ▲ | ▲ |
| Czech Republic | ▼ | ▼ | ▼ | ▼ | ▼ | | | | | | | | ▲ | ▲ | ▲ | ▲ | ▲ | ▲ | ▲ | ▲ | ▲ | ▲ | ▲ | ▲ | ▲ | ▲ | ▲ | ▲ | ▲ | ▲ | ▲ | ▲ | ▲ | ▲ | ▲ |
| New Zealand | ▼ | ▼ | ▼ | ▼ | ▼ | ▼ | ▼ | ▼ | ▼ | ▼ | ▼ | ▼ | | | | | | | | ▲ | ▲ | ▲ | ▲ | ▲ | ▲ | ▲ | ▲ | ▲ | ▲ | ▲ | ▲ | ▲ | ▲ | ▲ | ▲ |
| Scotland | ▼ | ▼ | ▼ | ▼ | ▼ | ▼ | ▼ | ▼ | ▼ | ▼ | ▼ | ▼ | | | | | | | | ▲ | ▲ | ▲ | ▲ | ▲ | ▲ | ▲ | ▲ | ▲ | ▲ | ▲ | ▲ | ▲ | ▲ | ▲ | ▲ |
| Singapore | ▼ | ▼ | ▼ | ▼ | ▼ | ▼ | ▼ | ▼ | ▼ | ▼ | ▼ | ▼ | | | | | | | | ▲ | ▲ | ▲ | ▲ | ▲ | ▲ | ▲ | ▲ | ▲ | ▲ | ▲ | ▲ | ▲ | ▲ | ▲ | ▲ |
| Russian Federation | ▼ | ▼ | ▼ | ▼ | ▼ | ▼ | ▼ | ▼ | ▼ | ▼ | ▼ | ▼ | | | | | | | | ▲ | ▲ | ▲ | ▲ | ▲ | ▲ | ▲ | ▲ | ▲ | ▲ | ▲ | ▲ | ▲ | ▲ | ▲ | ▲ |
| Hong Kong, SAR | ▼ | ▼ | ▼ | ▼ | ▼ | ▼ | ▼ | ▼ | ▼ | ▼ | ▼ | ▼ | | | | | | | | ▲ | ▲ | ▲ | ▲ | ▲ | ▲ | ▲ | ▲ | ▲ | ▲ | ▲ | ▲ | ▲ | ▲ | ▲ | ▲ |
| France | ▼ | ▼ | ▼ | ▼ | ▼ | ▼ | ▼ | ▼ | ▼ | ▼ | ▼ | ▼ | | | | | | | | | ▲ | ▲ | ▲ | ▲ | ▲ | ▲ | ▲ | ▲ | ▲ | ▲ | ▲ | ▲ | ▲ | ▲ | ▲ |
| Greece | ▼ | ▼ | ▼ | ▼ | ▼ | ▼ | ▼ | ▼ | ▼ | ▼ | ▼ | ▼ | | | | | | | | | ▲ | ▲ | ▲ | ▲ | ▲ | ▲ | ▲ | ▲ | ▲ | ▲ | ▲ | ▲ | ▲ | ▲ | ▲ |
| Slovak Republic | ▼ | ▼ | ▼ | ▼ | ▼ | ▼ | ▼ | ▼ | ▼ | ▼ | ▼ | ▼ | ▼ | ▼ | ▼ | ▼ | ▼ | | | | | | ▲ | ▲ | ▲ | ▲ | ▲ | ▲ | ▲ | ▲ | ▲ | ▲ | ▲ | ▲ | ▲ |
| Iceland | ▼ | ▼ | ▼ | ▼ | ▼ | ▼ | ▼ | ▼ | ▼ | ▼ | ▼ | ▼ | ▼ | ▼ | ▼ | ▼ | ▼ | ▼ | ▼ | | | | | ▲ | ▲ | ▲ | ▲ | ▲ | ▲ | ▲ | ▲ | ▲ | ▲ | ▲ | ▲ |
| Romania | ▼ | ▼ | ▼ | ▼ | ▼ | ▼ | ▼ | ▼ | ▼ | ▼ | ▼ | ▼ | ▼ | ▼ | ▼ | ▼ | ▼ | ▼ | ▼ | | | | | ▲ | ▲ | ▲ | ▲ | ▲ | ▲ | ▲ | ▲ | ▲ | ▲ | ▲ | ▲ |
| Israel | ▼ | ▼ | ▼ | ▼ | ▼ | ▼ | ▼ | ▼ | ▼ | ▼ | ▼ | ▼ | ▼ | ▼ | ▼ | ▼ | ▼ | ▼ | ▼ | ▼ | | | | | ▲ | ▲ | ▲ | ▲ | ▲ | ▲ | ▲ | ▲ | ▲ | ▲ | ▲ |
| Slovenia | ▼ | ▼ | ▼ | ▼ | ▼ | ▼ | ▼ | ▼ | ▼ | ▼ | ▼ | ▼ | ▼ | ▼ | ▼ | ▼ | ▼ | ▼ | ▼ | ▼ | ▼ | ▼ | | | | ▲ | ▲ | ▲ | ▲ | ▲ | ▲ | ▲ | ▲ | ▲ | ▲ |
| Norway | ▼ | ▼ | ▼ | ▼ | ▼ | ▼ | ▼ | ▼ | ▼ | ▼ | ▼ | ▼ | ▼ | ▼ | ▼ | ▼ | ▼ | ▼ | ▼ | ▼ | ▼ | ▼ | ▼ | | | | | ▲ | ▲ | ▲ | ▲ | ▲ | ▲ | ▲ | ▲ |
| Cyprus | ▼ | ▼ | ▼ | ▼ | ▼ | ▼ | ▼ | ▼ | ▼ | ▼ | ▼ | ▼ | ▼ | ▼ | ▼ | ▼ | ▼ | ▼ | ▼ | ▼ | ▼ | ▼ | ▼ | ▼ | | | | ▲ | ▲ | ▲ | ▲ | ▲ | ▲ | ▲ | ▲ |
| Moldova, Rep. of | ▼ | ▼ | ▼ | ▼ | ▼ | ▼ | ▼ | ▼ | ▼ | ▼ | ▼ | ▼ | ▼ | ▼ | ▼ | ▼ | ▼ | ▼ | ▼ | ▼ | ▼ | ▼ | ▼ | ▼ | | | | ▲ | ▲ | ▲ | ▲ | ▲ | ▲ | ▲ | ▲ |
| Turkey | ▼ | ▼ | ▼ | ▼ | ▼ | ▼ | ▼ | ▼ | ▼ | ▼ | ▼ | ▼ | ▼ | ▼ | ▼ | ▼ | ▼ | ▼ | ▼ | ▼ | ▼ | ▼ | ▼ | ▼ | ▼ | ▼ | ▼ | | | ▲ | ▲ | ▲ | ▲ | ▲ | ▲ |
| Macedonia, Rep. of | ▼ | ▼ | ▼ | ▼ | ▼ | ▼ | ▼ | ▼ | ▼ | ▼ | ▼ | ▼ | ▼ | ▼ | ▼ | ▼ | ▼ | ▼ | ▼ | ▼ | ▼ | ▼ | ▼ | ▼ | ▼ | ▼ | ▼ | | | | | ▲ | ▲ | ▲ | ▲ |
| Colombia | ▼ | ▼ | ▼ | ▼ | ▼ | ▼ | ▼ | ▼ | ▼ | ▼ | ▼ | ▼ | ▼ | ▼ | ▼ | ▼ | ▼ | ▼ | ▼ | ▼ | ▼ | ▼ | ▼ | ▼ | ▼ | ▼ | ▼ | ▼ | | | | | ▲ | ▲ | ▲ |
| Argentina | ▼ | ▼ | ▼ | ▼ | ▼ | ▼ | ▼ | ▼ | ▼ | ▼ | ▼ | ▼ | ▼ | ▼ | ▼ | ▼ | ▼ | ▼ | ▼ | ▼ | ▼ | ▼ | ▼ | ▼ | ▼ | ▼ | ▼ | ▼ | | | | | ▲ | ▲ | ▲ |
| Iran, Islamic Rep. of | ▼ | ▼ | ▼ | ▼ | ▼ | ▼ | ▼ | ▼ | ▼ | ▼ | ▼ | ▼ | ▼ | ▼ | ▼ | ▼ | ▼ | ▼ | ▼ | ▼ | ▼ | ▼ | ▼ | ▼ | ▼ | ▼ | ▼ | ▼ | ▼ | | | | ▲ | ▲ | ▲ |
| Kuwait | ▼ | ▼ | ▼ | ▼ | ▼ | ▼ | ▼ | ▼ | ▼ | ▼ | ▼ | ▼ | ▼ | ▼ | ▼ | ▼ | ▼ | ▼ | ▼ | ▼ | ▼ | ▼ | ▼ | ▼ | ▼ | ▼ | ▼ | ▼ | ▼ | ▼ | ▼ | ▼ | | | ▲ |
| Morocco | ▼ | ▼ | ▼ | ▼ | ▼ | ▼ | ▼ | ▼ | ▼ | ▼ | ▼ | ▼ | ▼ | ▼ | ▼ | ▼ | ▼ | ▼ | ▼ | ▼ | ▼ | ▼ | ▼ | ▼ | ▼ | ▼ | ▼ | ▼ | ▼ | ▼ | ▼ | ▼ | | | ▲ |
| Belize | ▼ | ▼ | ▼ | ▼ | ▼ | ▼ | ▼ | ▼ | ▼ | ▼ | ▼ | ▼ | ▼ | ▼ | ▼ | ▼ | ▼ | ▼ | ▼ | ▼ | ▼ | ▼ | ▼ | ▼ | ▼ | ▼ | ▼ | ▼ | ▼ | ▼ | ▼ | ▼ | ▼ | ▼ | |
| * Ontario (Canada) | ▼ | | | | | | | | | | ▲ | ▲ | ▲ | ▲ | ▲ | ▲ | ▲ | ▲ | ▲ | ▲ | ▲ | ▲ | ▲ | ▲ | ▲ | ▲ | ▲ | ▲ | ▲ | ▲ | ▲ | ▲ | ▲ | ▲ | ▲ |
| * Quebec (Canada) | ▼ | ▼ | ▼ | ▼ | ▼ | | | | | | | | | | | ▲ | ▲ | ▲ | ▲ | ▲ | ▲ | ▲ | ▲ | ▲ | ▲ | ▲ | ▲ | ▲ | ▲ | ▲ | ▲ | ▲ | ▲ | ▲ | ▲ |

▲  Average achievement significantly higher than comparison country

▼  Average achievement significantly lower than comparison country

\* Canada is represented by the provinces of Ontario and Quebec only. The international average does not include the results from these provinces separately.

Source: IEA Progress in International Reading Literacy Study (PIRLS) 2001

indicates that performance was significantly lower than the country listed across the top of the table. Absence of a symbol indicates no significant difference.

The figure illustrates how the listing of countries forms a series of blocks of countries which do not differ significantly among themselves, but are different from the blocks of countries above and below. Sweden had a mean score significantly greater than all other countries. Then The Netherlands, England and Bulgaria form a block which do not differ among themselves but have significantly higher scores than the next block, which includes Latvia, Canada, Lithuania, Hungary, United States, Italy and Germany.

For England, the figure shows that performance was only significantly worse than the top performing country, Sweden. There were no significant differences with The Netherlands or Bulgaria, and England was significantly better in reading achievement than all other countries. Hence, these included the English-speaking countries of the United States, New Zealand and Scotland. They also included the larger European countries of Italy, Germany and France. England also had an average score which was significantly greater than those for all the pre-accession European states except Bulgaria.

## 2.2 Reading for literacy experience and reading to acquire and use information

PIRLS 2001 calculated results by the two over-arching purposes for reading:

- reading for literary experience

- reading to acquire and use information.

In PIRLS, an equal proportion of material assessed each purpose. The literary texts were narrative fiction in the form of short stories. The informational texts represented a variety of chronological and non-chronological texts. The texts, submitted by and exhaustively reviewed by the participating countries, were selected from sources typical of those available to children in and out of school.

Figures 2.3 and 2.4 present the distributions of pupil achievement in reading for literary and informational purposes respectively. The form of the figures is similar to that of Figure 2.1, with the countries in order of average scale score and showing the 5th, 25th, 75th and 95th percentile as well as the 95 per cent confidence interval around the mean score. For each of the two purposes, the international average was scaled to 500, the same as the overall average.

Figure 2.3 shows that for literary purposes, Sweden and England had the highest reading achievement scale score, with an average of 559. Scores ranged down to 330 for Belize. Twenty-four countries were above the international average and 11 below it. English-speaking countries were all above average, as were the large European countries.

In reading for informational purposes (Figure 2.4), Sweden, The Netherlands and Bulgaria had the highest average achievement, with Sweden having significantly higher mean achievement than all other countries, with an average score of 559. Twenty-five countries were above the international average and ten below it, with scores ranging down to 332. The mean score for England was 546, resulting in a slightly lower position than for reading overall.

## Figure 2.3 Distribution of reading achievement for literary purposes

| Countries | Reading Achievement Scale Score | | Average Scale Score | Years of Formal Schooling | Average Age |
|---|---|---|---|---|---|
| Sweden | | ▲ | 559 (2.4) | 4 | 10.8 |
| †2a England | | ▲ | 559 (3.9) | 5 | 10.2 |
| † Netherlands | | ▲ | 552 (2.5) | 4 | 10.3 |
| † United States | | ▲ | 550 (3.8) | 4 | 10.2 |
| Bulgaria | | ▲ | 550 (3.9) | 4 | 10.9 |
| Hungary | | ▲ | 548 (2.0) | 4 | 10.7 |
| 1 Lithuania | | ▲ | 546 (3.1) | 4 | 10.9 |
| * 1 Canada (O,Q) | | ▲ | 545 (2.6) | 4 | 10.0 |
| Italy | | ▲ | 543 (2.7) | 4 | 9.8 |
| Latvia | | ▲ | 537 (2.2) | 4 | 11.0 |
| Germany | | ▲ | 537 (1.9) | 4 | 10.5 |
| Czech Republic | | ▲ | 535 (2.3) | 4 | 10.5 |
| New Zealand | | ▲ | 531 (3.9) | 5 | 10.1 |
| † Scotland | | ▲ | 529 (3.5) | 5 | 9.8 |
| Singapore | | ▲ | 528 (5.6) | 4 | 10.1 |
| 2a Greece | | ▲ | 528 (3.3) | 4 | 9.9 |
| 2a Russian Federation | | ▲ | 523 (3.9) | 3 or 4 | 10.3 |
| Iceland | | ▲ | 520 (1.3) | 4 | 9.7 |
| France | | ▲ | 518 (2.6) | 4 | 10.1 |
| Hong Kong, SAR | | ▲ | 518 (3.1) | 4 | 10.2 |
| Slovak Republic | | ▲ | 512 (2.6) | 4 | 10.3 |
| Romania | | ▲ | 512 (4.7) | 4 | 11.1 |
| 2b Israel | | ▲ | 510 (2.6) | 4 | 10.0 |
| Norway | | ▲ | 506 (2.7) | 4 | 10.0 |
| International Avg. | | | 500 (0.6) | 4 | 10.3 |
| Slovenia | | | 499 (1.8) | 3 | 9.8 |
| Cyprus | | | 498 (2.5) | 4 | 9.7 |
| Moldova, Rep. of | | ▼ | 480 (3.7) | 4 | 10.8 |
| Turkey | | ▼ | 448 (3.4) | 4 | 10.2 |
| Macedonia, Rep. of | | ▼ | 441 (4.5) | 4 | 10.7 |
| Colombia | | ▼ | 425 (4.2) | 4 | 10.5 |
| Iran, Islamic Rep. of | | ▼ | 421 (4.5) | 4 | 10.4 |
| Argentina | | ▼ | 419 (5.8) | 4 | 10.2 |
| Kuwait | | ▼ | 394 (3.8) | 4 | 9.9 |
| ‡ Morocco | | ▼ | 347 (8.4) | 4 | 11.2 |
| Belize | | ▼ | 330 (4.9) | 4 | 9.8 |
| * Ontario (Canada) | | ▲ | 551 (3.3) | 4 | 9.9 |
| * Quebec (Canada) | | ▲ | 534 (3.0) | 4 | 10.2 |

200  300  400  500  600  700  800

Percentiles of Performance
5th  25th  75th  95th

Average and 95% Confidence Interval (±2SE)

▲ Country average significantly higher than international average

▼ Country average significantly lower than international average

* Canada is represented by the provinces of Ontario and Quebec only. The international average does not include the results from these provinces separately.

† Met guidelines for sample participation rates only after replacement schools were included.

‡ Nearly satisfying guidelines for sample participation rates after replacement schools were included.

1 National Desired Population does not cover all of International Desired Population. Because coverage falls below 65%, Canada is annotated Canada (O, Q) for the provinces of Ontario and Quebec only.

2a National Defined Population covers less than 95% of National Desired Population.

2b National Defined Population covers less than 80% of National Desired Population.

( ) Standard errors appear in parentheses. Because results are rounded to the nearest whole number, some totals may appear inconsistent.

Source: IEA Progress in International Reading Literacy Study (PIRLS) 2001

## Figure 2.4 Distribution of reading achievement for informational purposes

| Countries | Reading Achievement Scale Score | | Average Scale Score | Years of Formal Schooling | Average Age |
|---|---|---|---|---|---|
| Sweden | | ⋏ | 559 (2.2) | 4 | 10.8 |
| † Netherlands | | ⋏ | 553 (2.6) | 4 | 10.3 |
| Bulgaria | | ⋏ | 551 (3.6) | 4 | 10.9 |
| Latvia | | ⋏ | 547 (2.3) | 4 | 11.0 |
| †2a England | | ⋏ | 546 (3.6) | 5 | 10.2 |
| * 1 Canada (O,Q) | | ⋏ | 541 (2.4) | 4 | 10.0 |
| 1 Lithuania | | ⋏ | 540 (2.7) | 4 | 10.9 |
| Germany | | ⋏ | 538 (1.9) | 4 | 10.5 |
| Hungary | | ⋏ | 537 (2.2) | 4 | 10.7 |
| Hong Kong, SAR | | ⋏ | 537 (2.9) | 4 | 10.2 |
| Czech Republic | | ⋏ | 536 (2.7) | 4 | 10.5 |
| Italy | | ⋏ | 536 (2.4) | 4 | 9.8 |
| † United States | | ⋏ | 533 (3.7) | 4 | 10.2 |
| France | | ⋏ | 533 (2.5) | 4 | 10.1 |
| 2a Russian Federation | | ⋏ | 531 (4.3) | 3 or 4 | 10.3 |
| Singapore | | ⋏ | 527 (4.8) | 4 | 10.1 |
| † Scotland | | ⋏ | 527 (3.6) | 5 | 9.8 |
| New Zealand | | ⋏ | 525 (3.8) | 5 | 10.1 |
| Slovak Republic | | ⋏ | 522 (2.7) | 4 | 10.3 |
| 2a Greece | | ⋏ | 521 (3.7) | 4 | 9.9 |
| Romania | | ⋏ | 512 (4.6) | 4 | 11.1 |
| 2b Israel | | ⋏ | 507 (2.9) | 4 | 10.0 |
| Moldova, Rep. of | | | 505 (4.7) | 4 | 10.8 |
| Iceland | | ⋏ | 504 (1.5) | 4 | 9.7 |
| Slovenia | | | 503 (1.9) | 3 | 9.8 |
| International Avg. | | | 500 (0.7) | 4 | 10.3 |
| Norway | | ⋎ | 492 (2.8) | 4 | 10.0 |
| Cyprus | | ⋎ | 490 (3.0) | 4 | 9.7 |
| Turkey | | ⋎ | 452 (3.8) | 4 | 10.2 |
| Macedonia, Rep. of | | ⋎ | 445 (5.2) | 4 | 10.7 |
| Colombia | | ⋎ | 424 (4.3) | 4 | 10.5 |
| Argentina | | ⋎ | 422 (5.4) | 4 | 10.2 |
| Iran, Islamic Rep. of | | ⋎ | 408 (4.6) | 4 | 10.4 |
| Kuwait | | ⋎ | 403 (4.5) | 4 | 9.9 |
| ‡ Morocco | | ⋎ | 358 (10.9) | 4 | 11.2 |
| Belize | | ⋎ | 332 (4.9) | 4 | 9.8 |
| | | | | | |
| * Ontario (Canada) | | ⋏ | 542 (3.2) | 4 | 9.9 |
| * Quebec (Canada) | | ⋏ | 541 (2.9) | 4 | 10.2 |

200   300   400   500   600   700   800

Percentiles of Performance
5th   25th   75th   95th

Average and 95% Confidence Interval (±2SE)

⋏ Country average significantly higher than international average

⋎ Country average significantly lower than international average

* Canada is represented by the provinces of Ontario and Quebec only. The international average does not include the results from these provinces separately.
† Met guidelines for sample participation rates only after replacement schools were included.
‡ Nearly satisfying guidelines for sample participation rates after replacement schools were included.
1 National Desired Population does not cover all of International Desired Population. Because coverage falls below 65%, Canada is annotated Canada (O, Q) for the provinces of Ontario and Quebec only.
2a National Defined Population covers less than 95% of National Desired Population.
2b National Defined Population covers less than 80% of National Desired Population.
( ) Standard errors appear in parentheses. Because results are rounded to the nearest whole number, some totals may appear inconsistent.

Source: IEA Progress in International Reading Literacy Study (PIRLS) 2001

The range in performance across the participating countries was nearly identical for the two purposes (229 scale-score points for literary compared to 227 for informational), and approximately the same number of countries performed significantly above and below the international average. In reading for literary purposes, 24 countries performed above the international average, two similar to it, and nine below it. In reading for informational purposes, 23 countries performed above the international average, two similar to it, and ten below it. However, while the ordering is similar for the two purposes and overall achievement, there are some interesting differences between literary and informational reading in the relative performance of the PIRLS countries.

**Figure 2.5  Multiple comparisons of average reading achievement for literary purposes**

Instructions: Read across the row for a country to compare performance with the countries listed along the top of the chart. The symbols indicate whether the average achievement of the country in the row is significantly lower than that of the comparison country, significantly higher than that of the comparison country, or if there is no statistically significant difference between the average achievement of the two countries.

| | Sweden | England | Netherlands | United States | Bulgaria | Hungary | Lithuania | Canada (O,Q) | Italy | Latvia | Germany | Czech Republic | New Zealand | Scotland | Singapore | Greece | Russian Federation | Iceland | France | Hong Kong, SAR | Slovak Republic | Romania | Israel | Norway | Slovenia | Cyprus | Moldova, Rep. of | Turkey | Macedonia, Rep. of | Colombia | Iran, Islamic Rep. of | Argentina | Kuwait | Morocco | Belize |
|---|---|---|---|---|---|---|---|---|---|---|---|---|---|---|---|---|---|---|---|---|---|---|---|---|---|---|---|---|---|---|---|---|---|---|---|
| Sweden | | ▲ | ▲ | ▲ | ▲ | ▲ | ▲ | ▲ | ▲ | ▲ | ▲ | ▲ | ▲ | ▲ | ▲ | ▲ | ▲ | ▲ | ▲ | ▲ | ▲ | ▲ | ▲ | ▲ | ▲ | ▲ | ▲ | ▲ | ▲ | ▲ | ▲ | ▲ | ▲ | ▲ | ▲ |
| England | | | | | | ▲ | ▲ | ▲ | ▲ | ▲ | ▲ | ▲ | ▲ | ▲ | ▲ | ▲ | ▲ | ▲ | ▲ | ▲ | ▲ | ▲ | ▲ | ▲ | ▲ | ▲ | ▲ | ▲ | ▲ | ▲ | ▲ | ▲ | ▲ | ▲ | ▲ |
| Netherlands | ▼ | | | | ▲ | ▲ | ▲ | ▲ | ▲ | ▲ | ▲ | ▲ | ▲ | ▲ | ▲ | ▲ | ▲ | ▲ | ▲ | ▲ | ▲ | ▲ | ▲ | ▲ | ▲ | ▲ | ▲ | ▲ | ▲ | ▲ | ▲ | ▲ | ▲ | ▲ | ▲ |
| United States | ▼ | | | | | ▲ | ▲ | ▲ | ▲ | ▲ | ▲ | ▲ | ▲ | ▲ | ▲ | ▲ | ▲ | ▲ | ▲ | ▲ | ▲ | ▲ | ▲ | ▲ | ▲ | ▲ | ▲ | ▲ | ▲ | ▲ | ▲ | ▲ | ▲ | ▲ | ▲ |
| Bulgaria | ▼ | | | | | ▲ | ▲ | ▲ | ▲ | ▲ | ▲ | ▲ | ▲ | ▲ | ▲ | ▲ | ▲ | ▲ | ▲ | ▲ | ▲ | ▲ | ▲ | ▲ | ▲ | ▲ | ▲ | ▲ | ▲ | ▲ | ▲ | ▲ | ▲ | ▲ | ▲ |
| Hungary | ▼ | ▼ | | | | | ▲ | ▲ | ▲ | ▲ | ▲ | ▲ | ▲ | ▲ | ▲ | ▲ | ▲ | ▲ | ▲ | ▲ | ▲ | ▲ | ▲ | ▲ | ▲ | ▲ | ▲ | ▲ | ▲ | ▲ | ▲ | ▲ | ▲ | ▲ | ▲ |
| Lithuania | ▼ | ▼ | | | | | | ▲ | ▲ | ▲ | ▲ | ▲ | ▲ | ▲ | ▲ | ▲ | ▲ | ▲ | ▲ | ▲ | ▲ | ▲ | ▲ | ▲ | ▲ | ▲ | ▲ | ▲ | ▲ | ▲ | ▲ | ▲ | ▲ | ▲ | ▲ |
| Canada (O,Q) | ▼ | ▼ | ▼ | | | | | | ▲ | ▲ | ▲ | ▲ | ▲ | ▲ | ▲ | ▲ | ▲ | ▲ | ▲ | ▲ | ▲ | ▲ | ▲ | ▲ | ▲ | ▲ | ▲ | ▲ | ▲ | ▲ | ▲ | ▲ | ▲ | ▲ | ▲ |
| Italy | ▼ | ▼ | ▼ | | | | | | | ▲ | ▲ | ▲ | ▲ | ▲ | ▲ | ▲ | ▲ | ▲ | ▲ | ▲ | ▲ | ▲ | ▲ | ▲ | ▲ | ▲ | ▲ | ▲ | ▲ | ▲ | ▲ | ▲ | ▲ | ▲ | ▲ |
| Latvia | ▼ | ▼ | ▼ | ▼ | ▼ | ▼ | ▼ | ▼ | | | ▲ | ▲ | ▲ | ▲ | ▲ | ▲ | ▲ | ▲ | ▲ | ▲ | ▲ | ▲ | ▲ | ▲ | ▲ | ▲ | ▲ | ▲ | ▲ | ▲ | ▲ | ▲ | ▲ | ▲ | ▲ |
| Germany | ▼ | ▼ | ▼ | ▼ | ▼ | ▼ | ▼ | ▼ | ▼ | | | ▲ | ▲ | ▲ | ▲ | ▲ | ▲ | ▲ | ▲ | ▲ | ▲ | ▲ | ▲ | ▲ | ▲ | ▲ | ▲ | ▲ | ▲ | ▲ | ▲ | ▲ | ▲ | ▲ | ▲ |
| Czech Republic | ▼ | ▼ | ▼ | ▼ | ▼ | ▼ | ▼ | ▼ | ▼ | | | | ▲ | ▲ | ▲ | ▲ | ▲ | ▲ | ▲ | ▲ | ▲ | ▲ | ▲ | ▲ | ▲ | ▲ | ▲ | ▲ | ▲ | ▲ | ▲ | ▲ | ▲ | ▲ | ▲ |
| New Zealand | ▼ | ▼ | ▼ | ▼ | ▼ | ▼ | ▼ | ▼ | ▼ | | | | | ▲ | ▲ | ▲ | ▲ | ▲ | ▲ | ▲ | ▲ | ▲ | ▲ | ▲ | ▲ | ▲ | ▲ | ▲ | ▲ | ▲ | ▲ | ▲ | ▲ | ▲ | ▲ |
| Scotland | ▼ | ▼ | ▼ | ▼ | ▼ | ▼ | ▼ | ▼ | ▼ | | | | | | ▲ | ▲ | ▲ | ▲ | ▲ | ▲ | ▲ | ▲ | ▲ | ▲ | ▲ | ▲ | ▲ | ▲ | ▲ | ▲ | ▲ | ▲ | ▲ | ▲ | ▲ |
| Singapore | ▼ | ▼ | ▼ | ▼ | ▼ | ▼ | ▼ | ▼ | ▼ | | | | | | | ▲ | ▲ | ▲ | ▲ | ▲ | ▲ | ▲ | ▲ | ▲ | ▲ | ▲ | ▲ | ▲ | ▲ | ▲ | ▲ | ▲ | ▲ | ▲ | ▲ |
| Greece | ▼ | ▼ | ▼ | ▼ | ▼ | ▼ | ▼ | ▼ | ▼ | ▼ | | | | | | | ▲ | ▲ | ▲ | ▲ | ▲ | ▲ | ▲ | ▲ | ▲ | ▲ | ▲ | ▲ | ▲ | ▲ | ▲ | ▲ | ▲ | ▲ | ▲ |
| Russian Federation | ▼ | ▼ | ▼ | ▼ | ▼ | ▼ | ▼ | ▼ | ▼ | ▼ | ▼ | ▼ | | | | | | ▲ | ▲ | ▲ | ▲ | ▲ | ▲ | ▲ | ▲ | ▲ | ▲ | ▲ | ▲ | ▲ | ▲ | ▲ | ▲ | ▲ | ▲ |
| Iceland | ▼ | ▼ | ▼ | ▼ | ▼ | ▼ | ▼ | ▼ | ▼ | ▼ | ▼ | ▼ | ▼ | ▼ | | | ▼ | | | ▲ | ▲ | ▲ | ▲ | ▲ | ▲ | ▲ | ▲ | ▲ | ▲ | ▲ | ▲ | ▲ | ▲ | ▲ | ▲ |
| France | ▼ | ▼ | ▼ | ▼ | ▼ | ▼ | ▼ | ▼ | ▼ | ▼ | ▼ | ▼ | ▼ | ▼ | | | ▼ | | | ▲ | ▲ | ▲ | ▲ | ▲ | ▲ | ▲ | ▲ | ▲ | ▲ | ▲ | ▲ | ▲ | ▲ | ▲ | ▲ |
| Hong Kong, SAR | ▼ | ▼ | ▼ | ▼ | ▼ | ▼ | ▼ | ▼ | ▼ | ▼ | ▼ | ▼ | ▼ | ▼ | ▼ | | ▼ | | | | ▲ | ▲ | ▲ | ▲ | ▲ | ▲ | ▲ | ▲ | ▲ | ▲ | ▲ | ▲ | ▲ | ▲ | ▲ |
| Slovak Republic | ▼ | ▼ | ▼ | ▼ | ▼ | ▼ | ▼ | ▼ | ▼ | ▼ | ▼ | ▼ | ▼ | ▼ | ▼ | ▼ | ▼ | ▼ | ▼ | | | | ▲ | ▲ | ▲ | ▲ | ▲ | ▲ | ▲ | ▲ | ▲ | ▲ | ▲ | ▲ | ▲ |
| Romania | ▼ | ▼ | ▼ | ▼ | ▼ | ▼ | ▼ | ▼ | ▼ | ▼ | ▼ | ▼ | ▼ | ▼ | ▼ | ▼ | | | | | | | ▲ | ▲ | ▲ | ▲ | ▲ | ▲ | ▲ | ▲ | ▲ | ▲ | ▲ | ▲ | ▲ |
| Israel | ▼ | ▼ | ▼ | ▼ | ▼ | ▼ | ▼ | ▼ | ▼ | ▼ | ▼ | ▼ | ▼ | ▼ | ▼ | ▼ | ▼ | ▼ | ▼ | ▼ | ▼ | ▼ | | | ▲ | ▲ | ▲ | ▲ | ▲ | ▲ | ▲ | ▲ | ▲ | ▲ | ▲ |
| Norway | ▼ | ▼ | ▼ | ▼ | ▼ | ▼ | ▼ | ▼ | ▼ | ▼ | ▼ | ▼ | ▼ | ▼ | ▼ | ▼ | ▼ | ▼ | ▼ | ▼ | ▼ | ▼ | | | ▲ | ▲ | ▲ | ▲ | ▲ | ▲ | ▲ | ▲ | ▲ | ▲ | ▲ |
| Slovenia | ▼ | ▼ | ▼ | ▼ | ▼ | ▼ | ▼ | ▼ | ▼ | ▼ | ▼ | ▼ | ▼ | ▼ | ▼ | ▼ | ▼ | ▼ | ▼ | ▼ | ▼ | ▼ | ▼ | ▼ | | | ▲ | ▲ | ▲ | ▲ | ▲ | ▲ | ▲ | ▲ | ▲ |
| Cyprus | ▼ | ▼ | ▼ | ▼ | ▼ | ▼ | ▼ | ▼ | ▼ | ▼ | ▼ | ▼ | ▼ | ▼ | ▼ | ▼ | ▼ | ▼ | ▼ | ▼ | ▼ | ▼ | ▼ | ▼ | | | ▲ | ▲ | ▲ | ▲ | ▲ | ▲ | ▲ | ▲ | ▲ |
| Moldova, Rep. of | ▼ | ▼ | ▼ | ▼ | ▼ | ▼ | ▼ | ▼ | ▼ | ▼ | ▼ | ▼ | ▼ | ▼ | ▼ | ▼ | ▼ | ▼ | ▼ | ▼ | ▼ | ▼ | ▼ | ▼ | ▼ | ▼ | | | ▲ | ▲ | ▲ | ▲ | ▲ | ▲ | ▲ |
| Turkey | ▼ | ▼ | ▼ | ▼ | ▼ | ▼ | ▼ | ▼ | ▼ | ▼ | ▼ | ▼ | ▼ | ▼ | ▼ | ▼ | ▼ | ▼ | ▼ | ▼ | ▼ | ▼ | ▼ | ▼ | ▼ | ▼ | | | ▲ | ▲ | ▲ | ▲ | ▲ | ▲ | ▲ |
| Macedonia, Rep. of | ▼ | ▼ | ▼ | ▼ | ▼ | ▼ | ▼ | ▼ | ▼ | ▼ | ▼ | ▼ | ▼ | ▼ | ▼ | ▼ | ▼ | ▼ | ▼ | ▼ | ▼ | ▼ | ▼ | ▼ | ▼ | ▼ | ▼ | ▼ | | | ▲ | ▲ | ▲ | ▲ | ▲ |
| Colombia | ▼ | ▼ | ▼ | ▼ | ▼ | ▼ | ▼ | ▼ | ▼ | ▼ | ▼ | ▼ | ▼ | ▼ | ▼ | ▼ | ▼ | ▼ | ▼ | ▼ | ▼ | ▼ | ▼ | ▼ | ▼ | ▼ | ▼ | ▼ | ▼ | | | ▲ | ▲ | ▲ | ▲ |
| Iran, Islamic Rep. of | ▼ | ▼ | ▼ | ▼ | ▼ | ▼ | ▼ | ▼ | ▼ | ▼ | ▼ | ▼ | ▼ | ▼ | ▼ | ▼ | ▼ | ▼ | ▼ | ▼ | ▼ | ▼ | ▼ | ▼ | ▼ | ▼ | ▼ | ▼ | ▼ | | | ▲ | ▲ | ▲ | ▲ |
| Argentina | ▼ | ▼ | ▼ | ▼ | ▼ | ▼ | ▼ | ▼ | ▼ | ▼ | ▼ | ▼ | ▼ | ▼ | ▼ | ▼ | ▼ | ▼ | ▼ | ▼ | ▼ | ▼ | ▼ | ▼ | ▼ | ▼ | ▼ | ▼ | ▼ | | | | ▲ | ▲ | ▲ |
| Kuwait | ▼ | ▼ | ▼ | ▼ | ▼ | ▼ | ▼ | ▼ | ▼ | ▼ | ▼ | ▼ | ▼ | ▼ | ▼ | ▼ | ▼ | ▼ | ▼ | ▼ | ▼ | ▼ | ▼ | ▼ | ▼ | ▼ | ▼ | ▼ | ▼ | ▼ | ▼ | | | ▲ | ▲ |
| Morocco | ▼ | ▼ | ▼ | ▼ | ▼ | ▼ | ▼ | ▼ | ▼ | ▼ | ▼ | ▼ | ▼ | ▼ | ▼ | ▼ | ▼ | ▼ | ▼ | ▼ | ▼ | ▼ | ▼ | ▼ | ▼ | ▼ | ▼ | ▼ | ▼ | ▼ | ▼ | ▼ | ▼ | | |
| Belize | ▼ | ▼ | ▼ | ▼ | ▼ | ▼ | ▼ | ▼ | ▼ | ▼ | ▼ | ▼ | ▼ | ▼ | ▼ | ▼ | ▼ | ▼ | ▼ | ▼ | ▼ | ▼ | ▼ | ▼ | ▼ | ▼ | ▼ | ▼ | ▼ | ▼ | ▼ | ▼ | ▼ | ▼ | |

| | | | | | | | | | | | | | | | | | | | | | | | | | | | | | | | | | | | |
|---|---|---|---|---|---|---|---|---|---|---|---|---|---|---|---|---|---|---|---|---|---|---|---|---|---|---|---|---|---|---|---|---|---|---|---|
| *Ontario (Canada) | ▼ | | | | | | ▲ | ▲ | ▲ | ▲ | ▲ | ▲ | ▲ | ▲ | ▲ | ▲ | ▲ | ▲ | ▲ | ▲ | ▲ | ▲ | ▲ | ▲ | ▲ | ▲ | ▲ | ▲ | ▲ | ▲ | ▲ | ▲ | ▲ | ▲ | ▲ |
| *Quebec (Canada) | ▼ | ▼ | ▼ | ▼ | ▼ | ▼ | ▼ | ▼ | ▼ | ▼ | | | | | ▲ | ▲ | ▲ | ▲ | ▲ | ▲ | ▲ | ▲ | ▲ | ▲ | ▲ | ▲ | ▲ | ▲ | ▲ | ▲ | ▲ | ▲ | ▲ | ▲ | ▲ |

▲ Average achievement significantly higher than comparison country

▼ Average achievement significantly lower than comparison country

\* Canada is represented by the provinces of Ontario and Quebec only. The international average does not include the results from these provinces separately.

Source: IEA Progress in International Reading Literacy Study (PIRLS) 2001

Figures 2.5 and 2.6 compare the mean reading achievement among pairs of individual countries for literary and informational purposes, respectively. These figures correspond to Figure 2.2 for overall reading achievement and are read the same way, by selecting a country and looking across the table. A chevron pointing upwards indicates significantly higher performance than the comparison country listed across the top; absence of a symbol indicates no significant difference; and a chevron pointing down indicates significantly lower performance.

In reading for literary purposes, Sweden and England had the highest average achievement, with Sweden having a significantly higher achievement score than all countries except England.

**Figure 2.6   Multiple comparisons of average reading achievement for informational purposes**

Instructions: Read across the row for a country to compare performance with the countries listed along the top of the chart. The symbols indicate whether the average achievement of the country in the row is significantly lower than that of the comparison country, significantly higher than that of the comparison country, or if there is no statistically significant difference between the average achievement of the two countries.

| | Sweden | Netherlands | Bulgaria | Latvia | England | Canada (O,Q) | Lithuania | Germany | Hungary | Hong Kong, SAR | Czech Republic | Italy | United States | France | Russian Federation | Singapore | Scotland | New Zealand | Slovak Republic | Greece | Romania | Israel | Moldova, Rep. of | Iceland | Slovenia | Norway | Cyprus | Turkey | Macedonia, Rep. of | Colombia | Argentina | Iran, Islamic Rep. of | Kuwait | Morocco | Belize |
|---|---|---|---|---|---|---|---|---|---|---|---|---|---|---|---|---|---|---|---|---|---|---|---|---|---|---|---|---|---|---|---|---|---|---|---|
| Sweden | | | ▲ | ▲ | ▲ | ▲ | ▲ | ▲ | ▲ | ▲ | ▲ | ▲ | ▲ | ▲ | ▲ | ▲ | ▲ | ▲ | ▲ | ▲ | ▲ | ▲ | ▲ | ▲ | ▲ | ▲ | ▲ | ▲ | ▲ | ▲ | ▲ | ▲ | ▲ | ▲ | ▲ |
| Netherlands | | | ▲ | ▲ | ▲ | ▲ | ▲ | ▲ | ▲ | ▲ | ▲ | ▲ | ▲ | ▲ | ▲ | ▲ | ▲ | ▲ | ▲ | ▲ | ▲ | ▲ | ▲ | ▲ | ▲ | ▲ | ▲ | ▲ | ▲ | ▲ | ▲ | ▲ | ▲ | ▲ | ▲ |
| Bulgaria | ▼ | ▼ | | ▲ | ▲ | ▲ | ▲ | ▲ | ▲ | ▲ | ▲ | ▲ | ▲ | ▲ | ▲ | ▲ | ▲ | ▲ | ▲ | ▲ | ▲ | ▲ | ▲ | ▲ | ▲ | ▲ | ▲ | ▲ | ▲ | ▲ | ▲ | ▲ | ▲ | ▲ | ▲ |
| Latvia | ▼ | ▼ | ▼ | | | ▲ | ▲ | ▲ | ▲ | ▲ | ▲ | ▲ | ▲ | ▲ | ▲ | ▲ | ▲ | ▲ | ▲ | ▲ | ▲ | ▲ | ▲ | ▲ | ▲ | ▲ | ▲ | ▲ | ▲ | ▲ | ▲ | ▲ | ▲ | ▲ | ▲ |
| England | ▼ | ▼ | ▼ | | | | | | | ▲ | ▲ | ▲ | ▲ | ▲ | ▲ | ▲ | ▲ | ▲ | ▲ | ▲ | ▲ | ▲ | ▲ | ▲ | ▲ | ▲ | ▲ | ▲ | ▲ | ▲ | ▲ | ▲ | ▲ | ▲ | ▲ |
| Canada (O,Q) | ▼ | ▼ | ▼ | ▼ | | | | | | | ▲ | ▲ | ▲ | ▲ | ▲ | ▲ | ▲ | ▲ | ▲ | ▲ | ▲ | ▲ | ▲ | ▲ | ▲ | ▲ | ▲ | ▲ | ▲ | ▲ | ▲ | ▲ | ▲ | ▲ | ▲ |
| Lithuania | ▼ | ▼ | ▼ | ▼ | | | | | | | | | | | | ▲ | ▲ | ▲ | ▲ | ▲ | ▲ | ▲ | ▲ | ▲ | ▲ | ▲ | ▲ | ▲ | ▲ | ▲ | ▲ | ▲ | ▲ | ▲ | ▲ |
| Germany | ▼ | ▼ | ▼ | ▼ | | | | | | | | | | | | ▲ | ▲ | ▲ | ▲ | ▲ | ▲ | ▲ | ▲ | ▲ | ▲ | ▲ | ▲ | ▲ | ▲ | ▲ | ▲ | ▲ | ▲ | ▲ | ▲ |
| Hungary | ▼ | ▼ | ▼ | ▼ | | | | | | | | | | | | ▲ | ▲ | ▲ | ▲ | ▲ | ▲ | ▲ | ▲ | ▲ | ▲ | ▲ | ▲ | ▲ | ▲ | ▲ | ▲ | ▲ | ▲ | ▲ | ▲ |
| Hong Kong, SAR | ▼ | ▼ | ▼ | ▼ | ▼ | | | | | | | | | | | ▲ | ▲ | ▲ | ▲ | ▲ | ▲ | ▲ | ▲ | ▲ | ▲ | ▲ | ▲ | ▲ | ▲ | ▲ | ▲ | ▲ | ▲ | ▲ | ▲ |
| Czech Republic | ▼ | ▼ | ▼ | ▼ | ▼ | ▼ | | | | | | | | | | ▲ | ▲ | ▲ | ▲ | ▲ | ▲ | ▲ | ▲ | ▲ | ▲ | ▲ | ▲ | ▲ | ▲ | ▲ | ▲ | ▲ | ▲ | ▲ | ▲ |
| Italy | ▼ | ▼ | ▼ | ▼ | ▼ | ▼ | | | | | | | | | | ▲ | ▲ | ▲ | ▲ | ▲ | ▲ | ▲ | ▲ | ▲ | ▲ | ▲ | ▲ | ▲ | ▲ | ▲ | ▲ | ▲ | ▲ | ▲ | ▲ |
| United States | ▼ | ▼ | ▼ | ▼ | ▼ | ▼ | | | | | | | | | | ▲ | ▲ | ▲ | ▲ | ▲ | ▲ | ▲ | ▲ | ▲ | ▲ | ▲ | ▲ | ▲ | ▲ | ▲ | ▲ | ▲ | ▲ | ▲ | ▲ |
| France | ▼ | ▼ | ▼ | ▼ | ▼ | ▼ | | | | | | | | | | ▲ | ▲ | ▲ | ▲ | ▲ | ▲ | ▲ | ▲ | ▲ | ▲ | ▲ | ▲ | ▲ | ▲ | ▲ | ▲ | ▲ | ▲ | ▲ | ▲ |
| Russian Federation | ▼ | ▼ | ▼ | ▼ | ▼ | ▼ | | | | | | | | | | ▲ | ▲ | ▲ | ▲ | ▲ | ▲ | ▲ | ▲ | ▲ | ▲ | ▲ | ▲ | ▲ | ▲ | ▲ | ▲ | ▲ | ▲ | ▲ | ▲ |
| Singapore | ▼ | ▼ | ▼ | ▼ | ▼ | ▼ | ▼ | ▼ | ▼ | ▼ | ▼ | ▼ | ▼ | ▼ | ▼ | | | | | | ▲ | ▲ | ▲ | ▲ | ▲ | ▲ | ▲ | ▲ | ▲ | ▲ | ▲ | ▲ | ▲ | ▲ | ▲ |
| Scotland | ▼ | ▼ | ▼ | ▼ | ▼ | ▼ | ▼ | ▼ | ▼ | ▼ | ▼ | ▼ | ▼ | ▼ | ▼ | | | | | | ▲ | ▲ | ▲ | ▲ | ▲ | ▲ | ▲ | ▲ | ▲ | ▲ | ▲ | ▲ | ▲ | ▲ | ▲ |
| New Zealand | ▼ | ▼ | ▼ | ▼ | ▼ | ▼ | ▼ | ▼ | ▼ | ▼ | ▼ | ▼ | ▼ | ▼ | ▼ | | | | | | ▲ | ▲ | ▲ | ▲ | ▲ | ▲ | ▲ | ▲ | ▲ | ▲ | ▲ | ▲ | ▲ | ▲ | ▲ |
| Slovak Republic | ▼ | ▼ | ▼ | ▼ | ▼ | ▼ | ▼ | ▼ | ▼ | ▼ | ▼ | ▼ | ▼ | ▼ | ▼ | | | | | | ▲ | ▲ | ▲ | ▲ | ▲ | ▲ | ▲ | ▲ | ▲ | ▲ | ▲ | ▲ | ▲ | ▲ | ▲ |
| Greece | ▼ | ▼ | ▼ | ▼ | ▼ | ▼ | ▼ | ▼ | ▼ | ▼ | ▼ | ▼ | ▼ | ▼ | ▼ | | | | | | ▲ | ▲ | ▲ | ▲ | ▲ | ▲ | ▲ | ▲ | ▲ | ▲ | ▲ | ▲ | ▲ | ▲ | ▲ |
| Romania | ▼ | ▼ | ▼ | ▼ | ▼ | ▼ | ▼ | ▼ | ▼ | ▼ | ▼ | ▼ | ▼ | ▼ | ▼ | ▼ | ▼ | ▼ | ▼ | ▼ | | | | | | ▲ | ▲ | ▲ | ▲ | ▲ | ▲ | ▲ | ▲ | ▲ | ▲ |
| Israel | ▼ | ▼ | ▼ | ▼ | ▼ | ▼ | ▼ | ▼ | ▼ | ▼ | ▼ | ▼ | ▼ | ▼ | ▼ | ▼ | ▼ | ▼ | ▼ | ▼ | | | | | | ▲ | ▲ | ▲ | ▲ | ▲ | ▲ | ▲ | ▲ | ▲ | ▲ |
| Moldova, Rep. of | ▼ | ▼ | ▼ | ▼ | ▼ | ▼ | ▼ | ▼ | ▼ | ▼ | ▼ | ▼ | ▼ | ▼ | ▼ | ▼ | ▼ | ▼ | ▼ | ▼ | | | | | | ▲ | ▲ | ▲ | ▲ | ▲ | ▲ | ▲ | ▲ | ▲ | ▲ |
| Iceland | ▼ | ▼ | ▼ | ▼ | ▼ | ▼ | ▼ | ▼ | ▼ | ▼ | ▼ | ▼ | ▼ | ▼ | ▼ | ▼ | ▼ | ▼ | ▼ | ▼ | | | | | | ▲ | ▲ | ▲ | ▲ | ▲ | ▲ | ▲ | ▲ | ▲ | ▲ |
| Slovenia | ▼ | ▼ | ▼ | ▼ | ▼ | ▼ | ▼ | ▼ | ▼ | ▼ | ▼ | ▼ | ▼ | ▼ | ▼ | ▼ | ▼ | ▼ | ▼ | ▼ | | | | | | ▲ | ▲ | ▲ | ▲ | ▲ | ▲ | ▲ | ▲ | ▲ | ▲ |
| Norway | ▼ | ▼ | ▼ | ▼ | ▼ | ▼ | ▼ | ▼ | ▼ | ▼ | ▼ | ▼ | ▼ | ▼ | ▼ | ▼ | ▼ | ▼ | ▼ | ▼ | ▼ | ▼ | ▼ | ▼ | ▼ | | | | ▲ | ▲ | ▲ | ▲ | ▲ | ▲ | ▲ |
| Cyprus | ▼ | ▼ | ▼ | ▼ | ▼ | ▼ | ▼ | ▼ | ▼ | ▼ | ▼ | ▼ | ▼ | ▼ | ▼ | ▼ | ▼ | ▼ | ▼ | ▼ | ▼ | ▼ | ▼ | ▼ | ▼ | | | | ▲ | ▲ | ▲ | ▲ | ▲ | ▲ | ▲ |
| Turkey | ▼ | ▼ | ▼ | ▼ | ▼ | ▼ | ▼ | ▼ | ▼ | ▼ | ▼ | ▼ | ▼ | ▼ | ▼ | ▼ | ▼ | ▼ | ▼ | ▼ | ▼ | ▼ | ▼ | ▼ | ▼ | | | | ▲ | ▲ | ▲ | ▲ | ▲ | ▲ | ▲ |
| Macedonia, Rep. of | ▼ | ▼ | ▼ | ▼ | ▼ | ▼ | ▼ | ▼ | ▼ | ▼ | ▼ | ▼ | ▼ | ▼ | ▼ | ▼ | ▼ | ▼ | ▼ | ▼ | ▼ | ▼ | ▼ | ▼ | ▼ | ▼ | ▼ | ▼ | | | ▲ | ▲ | ▲ | ▲ | ▲ |
| Colombia | ▼ | ▼ | ▼ | ▼ | ▼ | ▼ | ▼ | ▼ | ▼ | ▼ | ▼ | ▼ | ▼ | ▼ | ▼ | ▼ | ▼ | ▼ | ▼ | ▼ | ▼ | ▼ | ▼ | ▼ | ▼ | ▼ | ▼ | ▼ | | | ▲ | ▲ | ▲ | ▲ | ▲ |
| Argentina | ▼ | ▼ | ▼ | ▼ | ▼ | ▼ | ▼ | ▼ | ▼ | ▼ | ▼ | ▼ | ▼ | ▼ | ▼ | ▼ | ▼ | ▼ | ▼ | ▼ | ▼ | ▼ | ▼ | ▼ | ▼ | ▼ | ▼ | ▼ | ▼ | ▼ | | ▲ | ▲ | ▲ | ▲ |
| Iran, Islamic Rep. of | ▼ | ▼ | ▼ | ▼ | ▼ | ▼ | ▼ | ▼ | ▼ | ▼ | ▼ | ▼ | ▼ | ▼ | ▼ | ▼ | ▼ | ▼ | ▼ | ▼ | ▼ | ▼ | ▼ | ▼ | ▼ | ▼ | ▼ | ▼ | ▼ | ▼ | ▼ | | ▲ | ▲ | ▲ |
| Kuwait | ▼ | ▼ | ▼ | ▼ | ▼ | ▼ | ▼ | ▼ | ▼ | ▼ | ▼ | ▼ | ▼ | ▼ | ▼ | ▼ | ▼ | ▼ | ▼ | ▼ | ▼ | ▼ | ▼ | ▼ | ▼ | ▼ | ▼ | ▼ | ▼ | ▼ | ▼ | ▼ | | ▲ | ▲ |
| Morocco | ▼ | ▼ | ▼ | ▼ | ▼ | ▼ | ▼ | ▼ | ▼ | ▼ | ▼ | ▼ | ▼ | ▼ | ▼ | ▼ | ▼ | ▼ | ▼ | ▼ | ▼ | ▼ | ▼ | ▼ | ▼ | ▼ | ▼ | ▼ | ▼ | ▼ | ▼ | ▼ | ▼ | | ▲ |
| Belize | ▼ | ▼ | ▼ | ▼ | ▼ | ▼ | ▼ | ▼ | ▼ | ▼ | ▼ | ▼ | ▼ | ▼ | ▼ | ▼ | ▼ | ▼ | ▼ | ▼ | ▼ | ▼ | ▼ | ▼ | ▼ | ▼ | ▼ | ▼ | ▼ | ▼ | ▼ | ▼ | ▼ | ▼ | |
| * Ontario (Canada) | ▼ | ▼ | ▼ | | | | | | | | ▲ | | | | | ▲ | ▲ | ▲ | ▲ | ▲ | ▲ | ▲ | ▲ | ▲ | ▲ | ▲ | ▲ | ▲ | ▲ | ▲ | ▲ | ▲ | ▲ | ▲ | ▲ |
| * Quebec (Canada) | ▼ | ▼ | ▼ | | | | | | | | ▲ | | | | | ▲ | ▲ | ▲ | ▲ | ▲ | ▲ | ▲ | ▲ | ▲ | ▲ | ▲ | ▲ | ▲ | ▲ | ▲ | ▲ | ▲ | ▲ | ▲ | ▲ |

▲  Average achievement significantly higher than comparison country

▼  Average achievement significantly lower than comparison country

\*   Canada is represented by the provinces of Ontario and Quebec only. The international average does not include the results from these provinces separately.

Source: IEA Progress in International Reading Literacy Study (PIRLS) 2001

England performed significantly better than all other countries except The Netherlands, the United States and Bulgaria. Hence scores were higher than the English-speaking countries of Scotland and New Zealand and the large European countries of Italy, France and Germany.

In reading for informational purposes, Sweden, The Netherlands and Bulgaria had the highest average achievement, with Sweden having significantly higher mean achievement than all others, except these two. England, although it had a lower ranking than for literary purposes, did very well. Only Sweden gained a significantly higher average score. England had a significantly higher score than most other countries, including the United States, Scotland and New Zealand as English-speaking comparators, and Italy and France as large European countries. The average score did not differ significantly from that for Germany.

Figure 2.7 displays the difference between average achievement in the literary and informational purposes for each country. Many countries performed significantly better in one purpose compared to the other. Those at the top of the figure were better in literary purposes and those at the bottom were better in informational purposes. A darkened bar indicates that the difference was statistically significant. Countries with significantly higher performance in reading for literary purposes included the United States, Iceland, Norway, England, Italy and New Zealand. The difference for Scotland was in the same direction but did not quite reach significance. Other countries, including the Russian Federation and France, had significantly higher performance for reading for informational purposes.

Differences in relative performance may be related to one or more of a number of factors, such as: emphases in the intended curriculum or in widely used textbooks; strengths or weaknesses in curriculum implementation and the grade or age at which reading comprehension strategies are introduced. It is interesting to note that all the English-speaking countries favoured literary reading. The highest scoring countries, Sweden and The Netherlands, had little or no difference between the purposes. France, in contrast to the English-speaking countries, strongly favoured informational purposes for reading.

In England, the national literacy strategy has recently placed a strong emphasis on reading for information as well as on reading for literary purposes. In an international context, as seen by the performance of pupils, this is not yet reflected by the results for England which favoured reading for literary purposes. Although contained in the National Curriculum since 1989, active teaching of non-fiction texts has become more widespread with the national literacy strategy. Non-fiction books for young children have also been relatively rare. Data presented in Chapter 6 shows that the use of textbooks tends to be greater in other countries.

## 2.3  Range in performance

As indicated above, visual inspection of the range of performance from the 5th to 95th percentiles indicates that England has one of the largest ranges.

Table 2.1 shows the percentiles of achievement in reading for all the countries participating in PIRLS 2001. The countries with the widest range tend to be those with low average scores (Morocco, Belize, Macedonia). Indeed there is a high negative correlation between scores at the 5th percentile and the range, that is countries with a wide range of achievement tend to have low scores for their lowest performing pupils. This may indicate a slight ceiling effect (a bunching of scores at the upper end) in the tests for countries with overall high levels of achievement.

## Figure 2.7 Relative difference in performance between literary and informational purposes

| Countries | Literary Average Scale Score | Informational Average Scale Score | Relative Difference | Relative Difference Literary Higher | Relative Difference Informational Higher |
|---|---|---|---|---|---|
| † United States | 550 (3.8) | 533 (3.7) | 17 (1.2) | | |
| Iceland | 520 (1.3) | 504 (1.5) | 16 (1.3) | | |
| Norway | 506 (2.7) | 492 (2.8) | 14 (1.3) | | |
| †2a England | 559 (3.9) | 546 (3.6) | 14 (1.8) | | |
| Iran, Islamic Rep. of | 421 (4.5) | 408 (4.6) | 12 (1.9) | | |
| Hungary | 548 (2.0) | 537 (2.2) | 11 (1.1) | | |
| Cyprus | 498 (2.5) | 490 (3.0) | 8 (1.2) | | |
| Italy | 543 (2.7) | 536 (2.4) | 7 (1.2) | | |
| 2a Greece | 528 (3.3) | 521 (3.7) | 7 (1.7) | | |
| New Zealand | 531 (3.9) | 525 (3.8) | 7 (2.2) | | |
| 1 Lithuania | 546 (3.1) | 540 (2.7) | 6 (2.3) | | |
| 2b Israel | 510 (2.6) | 507 (2.9) | 3 (0.9) | | |
| * 1 Canada (O,Q) | 545 (2.6) | 541 (2.4) | 3 (1.6) | | |
| † Scotland | 529 (3.5) | 527 (3.6) | 2 (1.5) | | |
| Colombia | 425 (4.2) | 424 (4.3) | 2 (1.3) | | |
| Singapore | 528 (5.6) | 527 (4.8) | 1 (1.1) | | |
| Sweden | 559 (2.4) | 559 (2.2) | 1 (1.1) | | |
| International Avg. | 500 (0.6) | 500 (0.7) | 0 (0.2) | | |
| † Netherlands | 552 (2.5) | 553 (2.6) | 1 (0.9) | | |
| Romania | 512 (4.7) | 512 (4.6) | 1 (1.5) | | |
| Czech Republic | 535 (2.3) | 536 (2.7) | 1 (1.7) | | |
| Germany | 537 (1.9) | 538 (1.9) | 2 (1.3) | | |
| Bulgaria | 550 (3.9) | 551 (3.6) | 2 (1.6) | | |
| Belize | 330 (4.9) | 332 (4.9) | 3 (2.5) | | |
| Argentina | 419 (5.8) | 422 (5.4) | 3 (1.8) | | |
| Turkey | 448 (3.4) | 452 (3.8) | 4 (1.4) | | |
| Slovenia | 499 (1.8) | 503 (1.9) | 4 (1.3) | | |
| Macedonia, Rep. of | 441 (4.5) | 445 (5.2) | 4 (1.5) | | |
| 2a Russian Federation | 523 (3.9) | 531 (4.3) | 8 (1.7) | | |
| Kuwait | 394 (3.8) | 403 (4.5) | 9 (1.4) | | |
| Latvia | 537 (2.2) | 547 (2.3) | 10 (1.9) | | |
| Slovak Republic | 512 (2.6) | 522 (2.7) | 10 (1.3) | | |
| ‡ Morocco | 347 (8.4) | 358 (10.9) | 11 (3.7) | | |
| France | 518 (2.6) | 533 (2.5) | 15 (1.2) | | |
| Hong Kong, SAR | 518 (3.1) | 537 (2.9) | 20 (0.9) | | |
| Moldova, Rep. of | 480 (3.7) | 505 (4.7) | 25 (1.9) | | |
| | | | | | |
| * Ontario (Canada) | 551 (3.3) | 542 (3.2) | 10 (1.3) | | |
| * Quebec (Canada) | 534 (3.0) | 541 (2.9) | 7 (1.8) | | |

40     20     0     20     40

■ Difference statistically significant

* Canada is represented by the provinces of Ontario and Quebec only. The international average does not include the results from these provinces separately.
† Met guidelines for sample participation rates only after replacement schools were included.
‡ Nearly satisfying guidelines for sample participation rates after replacement schools were included.
1 National Desired Population does not cover all of International Desired Population. Because coverage falls below 65%, Canada is annotated Canada (O, Q) for the provinces of Ontario and Quebec only.
2a National Defined Population covers less than 95% of National Desired Population.
2b National Defined Population covers less than 80% of National Desired Population.
( ) Standard errors appear in parentheses. Because results are rounded to the nearest whole number, some totals may appear inconsistent.

Source: IEA Progress in International Reading Literacy Study (PIRLS) 2001

**Table 2.1   Percentiles of achievement in reading**

| Countries | 5th Percentile | 25th Percentile | 50th Percentile | 75th Percentile | 95th Percentile |
|---|---|---|---|---|---|
| Argentina | 257 (6.7) | 353 (8.7) | 424 (6.7) | 487 (6.5) | 571 (7.7) |
| Belize | 161 (3.4) | 251 (5.7) | 322 (4.8) | 401 (5.9) | 506 (5.3) |
| Bulgaria | 400 (11.9) | 502 (4.5) | 559 (3.7) | 607 (2.1) | 671 (3.8) |
| Canada (O,Q) | 419 (4.4) | 498 (2.7) | 547 (2.6) | 594 (5.1) | 658 (2.3) |
| Colombia | 287 (8.6) | 368 (5.9) | 424 (5.1) | 479 (6.4) | 551 (6.9) |
| Cyprus | 352 (4.3) | 441 (3.1) | 500 (3.2) | 551 (4.7) | 619 (5.0) |
| Czech Republic | 421 (5.2) | 496 (1.9) | 542 (2.7) | 582 (3.0) | 634 (4.7) |
| England | 395 (6.3) | 501 (4.4) | 559 (4.6) | 612 (4.5) | 685 (5.3) |
| France | 403 (5.2) | 481 (2.8) | 528 (2.1) | 573 (1.8) | 636 (4.5) |
| Germany | 419 (3.9) | 497 (3.1) | 544 (2.6) | 586 (1.9) | 640 (1.9) |
| Greece | 396 (4.0) | 477 (5.3) | 528 (4.5) | 576 (3.1) | 636 (4.1) |
| Hong Kong, SAR | 415 (6.4) | 491 (5.0) | 533 (3.9) | 571 (4.0) | 622 (3.2) |
| Hungary | 428 (4.4) | 502 (2.4) | 548 (3.8) | 589 (2.9) | 643 (3.8) |
| Iceland | 380 (3.3) | 466 (2.8) | 517 (1.9) | 564 (2.3) | 629 (5.4) |
| Iran, Islamic Rep. of | 260 (3.5) | 348 (6.0) | 416 (6.7) | 482 (4.7) | 560 (4.7) |
| Israel | 338 (7.0) | 450 (3.9) | 520 (2.8) | 575 (3.8) | 646 (4.2) |
| Italy | 415 (6.5) | 496 (3.2) | 546 (2.2) | 590 (3.1) | 649 (2.7) |
| Kuwait | 244 (7.6) | 335 (5.5) | 401 (5.0) | 461 (3.9) | 535 (5.3) |
| Latvia | 440 (4.9) | 505 (3.3) | 548 (2.7) | 586 (2.4) | 640 (3.4) |
| Lithuania | 433 (4.4) | 502 (4.0) | 547 (3.6) | 589 (2.3) | 642 (3.6) |
| Macedonia, Rep. of | 262 (8.3) | 368 (11.4) | 451 (5.5) | 520 (4.2) | 595 (2.5) |
| Moldova, Rep. of | 359 (5.0) | 445 (6.2) | 495 (5.0) | 544 (4.3) | 609 (6.4) |
| Morocco | 168 (8.7) | 266 (8.7) | 346 (11.0) | 428 (9.9) | 540 (21.2) |
| Netherlands | 458 (4.1) | 517 (3.8) | 556 (2.5) | 593 (2.9) | 645 (3.6) |
| New Zealand | 360 (4.7) | 472 (5.9) | 537 (3.6) | 593 (4.5) | 668 (5.1) |
| Norway | 351 (5.0) | 450 (4.1) | 507 (2.5) | 556 (2.8) | 620 (6.0) |
| Romania | 351 (13.4) | 456 (4.4) | 520 (3.6) | 574 (6.4) | 647 (4.4) |
| Russian Federation | 412 (12.9) | 488 (5.1) | 533 (3.4) | 574 (4.6) | 627 (4.0) |
| Scotland | 378 (5.1) | 476 (6.0) | 534 (3.4) | 586 (2.7) | 658 (6.1) |
| Singapore | 348 (10.6) | 479 (7.2) | 540 (4.6) | 592 (4.6) | 658 (5.4) |
| Slovak Republic | 389 (9.7) | 477 (2.7) | 525 (2.2) | 566 (1.8) | 623 (3.9) |
| Slovenia | 373 (6.4) | 456 (2.8) | 506 (2.5) | 551 (2.7) | 611 (3.0) |
| Sweden | 445 (4.5) | 521 (4.7) | 565 (2.4) | 605 (1.7) | 663 (2.1) |
| Turkey | 302 (3.9) | 392 (4.0) | 452 (3.8) | 510 (4.1) | 586 (6.0) |
| United States | 389 (8.9) | 492 (4.7) | 551 (2.8) | 601 (4.2) | 663 (2.8) |

( ) Standard errors appear in parentheses.

Some countries with wide ranges, such as Singapore, have a large proportion of pupils who are being educated and tested in a language other than that they speak at home. However, several developed English-speaking countries (New Zealand, England, Scotland and the United States) also tend to have a wide range of achievement. This contrasts with such European countries as Italy, France, Germany, Sweden and The Netherlands, which all have fairly narrow ranges of achievement. In particular The Netherlands forms a strong contrast with England, in that both have a very high average score, but The Netherlands has a range of 187 scale points from the 5th to 95th percentile, the smallest of all countries, whereas England has a range of 290 scale points.

An alternative manner of approaching this data is provided by Figure 2.8. This shows the percentages of pupils reaching three international benchmarks for PIRLS 2001. These are the top

10 per cent, the top 25 per cent (upper quartile) and the top 50 per cent (median) benchmarks. A description of the capabilities of children at these benchmarks is given in Chapter 4. The figure is ordered in terms of the percentages of pupils at the top 10 per cent benchmark. On this measure, England has the highest proportion of pupils in the top 10 per cent internationally. Similarly it has the second highest proportion in the top 25 per cent internationally, and the third highest proportion

**Figure 2.8   Percentage of students reaching PIRLS international benchmarks in reading achievement**

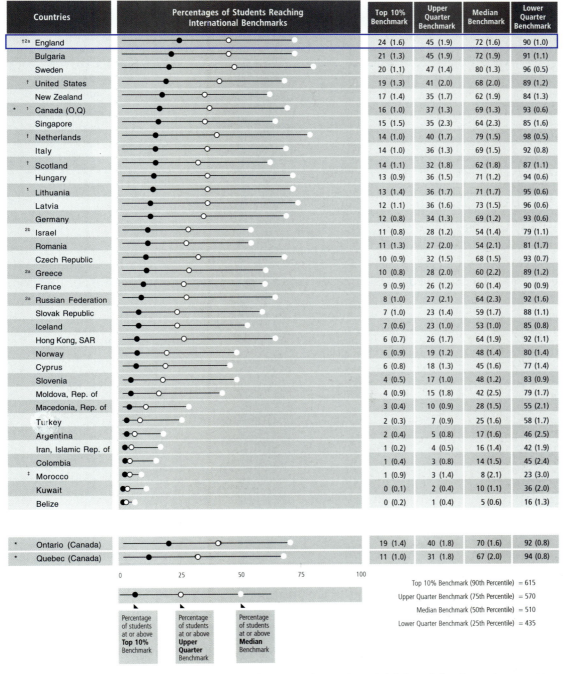

| Countries | Percentages of Students Reaching International Benchmarks | Top 10% Benchmark | Upper Quarter Benchmark | Median Benchmark | Lower Quarter Benchmark |
|---|---|---|---|---|---|
| †2a England | | 24 (1.6) | 45 (1.9) | 72 (1.6) | 90 (1.0) |
| Bulgaria | | 21 (1.3) | 45 (1.9) | 72 (1.9) | 91 (1.1) |
| Sweden | | 20 (1.1) | 47 (1.4) | 80 (1.3) | 96 (0.5) |
| † United States | | 19 (1.3) | 41 (2.0) | 68 (2.0) | 89 (1.2) |
| New Zealand | | 17 (1.4) | 35 (1.7) | 62 (1.9) | 84 (1.3) |
| * 1 Canada (O,Q) | | 16 (1.0) | 37 (1.3) | 69 (1.3) | 93 (0.6) |
| Singapore | | 15 (1.5) | 35 (2.3) | 64 (2.3) | 85 (1.6) |
| † Netherlands | | 14 (1.0) | 40 (1.7) | 79 (1.5) | 98 (0.5) |
| Italy | | 14 (1.0) | 36 (1.3) | 69 (1.5) | 92 (0.8) |
| † Scotland | | 14 (1.1) | 32 (1.8) | 62 (1.8) | 87 (1.1) |
| Hungary | | 13 (0.9) | 36 (1.5) | 71 (1.2) | 94 (0.6) |
| 1 Lithuania | | 13 (1.4) | 36 (1.7) | 71 (1.7) | 95 (0.6) |
| Latvia | | 12 (1.1) | 36 (1.6) | 73 (1.5) | 96 (0.6) |
| Germany | | 12 (0.8) | 34 (1.3) | 69 (1.2) | 93 (0.6) |
| 2b Israel | | 11 (0.8) | 28 (1.2) | 54 (1.4) | 79 (1.1) |
| Romania | | 11 (1.3) | 27 (2.0) | 54 (2.1) | 81 (1.7) |
| Czech Republic | | 10 (0.9) | 32 (1.5) | 68 (1.5) | 93 (0.7) |
| 2a Greece | | 10 (0.8) | 28 (2.0) | 60 (2.2) | 89 (1.2) |
| France | | 9 (0.9) | 26 (1.2) | 60 (1.4) | 90 (0.9) |
| 2a Russian Federation | | 8 (1.0) | 27 (2.1) | 64 (2.3) | 92 (1.6) |
| Slovak Republic | | 7 (1.0) | 23 (1.4) | 59 (1.7) | 88 (1.1) |
| Iceland | | 7 (0.6) | 23 (1.0) | 53 (1.0) | 85 (0.8) |
| Hong Kong, SAR | | 6 (0.7) | 26 (1.7) | 64 (1.9) | 92 (1.1) |
| Norway | | 6 (0.9) | 19 (1.2) | 48 (1.4) | 80 (1.4) |
| Cyprus | | 6 (0.8) | 18 (1.3) | 45 (1.6) | 77 (1.4) |
| Slovenia | | 4 (0.5) | 17 (1.0) | 48 (1.2) | 83 (0.9) |
| Moldova, Rep. of | | 4 (0.9) | 15 (1.8) | 42 (2.5) | 79 (1.7) |
| Macedonia, Rep. of | | 3 (0.4) | 10 (0.9) | 28 (1.5) | 55 (2.1) |
| Turkey | | 2 (0.3) | 7 (0.9) | 25 (1.6) | 58 (1.7) |
| Argentina | | 2 (0.4) | 5 (0.8) | 17 (1.6) | 46 (2.5) |
| Iran, Islamic Rep. of | | 1 (0.2) | 4 (0.5) | 16 (1.4) | 42 (1.9) |
| Colombia | | 1 (0.4) | 3 (0.8) | 14 (1.5) | 45 (2.4) |
| ‡ Morocco | | 1 (0.9) | 3 (1.4) | 8 (2.1) | 23 (3.0) |
| Kuwait | | 0 (0.1) | 2 (0.4) | 10 (1.1) | 36 (2.0) |
| Belize | | 0 (0.2) | 1 (0.4) | 5 (0.6) | 16 (1.3) |
| | | | | | |
| * Ontario (Canada) | | 19 (1.4) | 40 (1.8) | 70 (1.6) | 92 (0.8) |
| * Quebec (Canada) | | 11 (1.0) | 31 (1.8) | 67 (2.0) | 94 (0.8) |

Percentage of students at or above **Top 10% Benchmark**
Percentage of students at or above **Upper Quarter Benchmark**
Percentage of students at or above **Median Benchmark**

Top 10% Benchmark (90th Percentile) = 615
Upper Quarter Benchmark (75th Percentile) = 570
Median Benchmark (50th Percentile) = 510
Lower Quarter Benchmark (25th Percentile) = 435

\* Canada is represented by the provinces of Ontario and Quebec only. The international average does not include the results from these provinces separately.
† Met guidelines for sample participation rates only after replacement schools were included.
‡ Nearly satisfying guidelines for sample participation rates after replacement schools were included.
1 National Desired Population does not cover all of International Desired Population. Because coverage falls below 65%, Canada is annotated Canada (O, Q) for the provinces of Ontario and Quebec only.
2a National Defined Population covers less than 95% of National Desired Population.
2b National Defined Population covers less than 80% of National Desired Population.
( ) Standard errors appear in parentheses. Because results are rounded to the nearest whole number, some totals may appear inconsistent.

Source: IEA Progress in International Reading Literacy Study (PIRLS) 2001

in the top 50 per cent internationally. All of this data indicates that the top performing pupils in England are among the best in the world. They surpass the performance of other English-speaking countries and of the larger European countries, being matched or surpassed only by the children of Sweden, and perhaps The Netherlands.

**Figure 2.9  Standardised deviation from average of all countries for European countries**

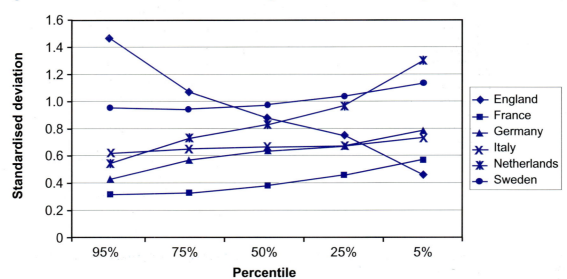

**Figure 2.10  Standardised deviation from average of all countries for countries testing in English**

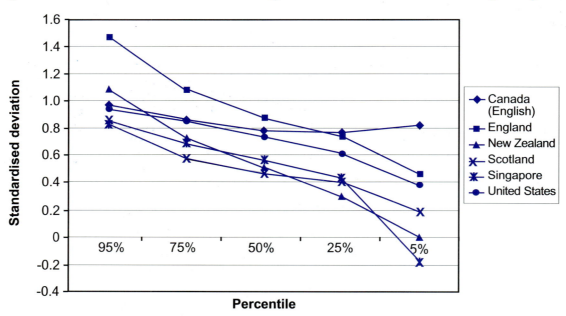

However, the reading performance of lower scoring pupils is not as encouraging. This is indicated by the large range of scores for England, referred to above. It can also be shown by expressing the data for Table 2.1 graphically.

Figure 2.9 shows the standardised results[2] of the large European countries. This illustrates that England has the highest scoring pupils at the 95th and 75th percentiles, but slips

---

2   For this purpose, standardised results have been calculated separately for each of the percentiles shown. This has been done by finding the mean and standard deviation in achievement scores across all the countries, then expressing each country's score as a proportion of the standard deviation above (positive figures) or below (negative) the international mean.

markedly at the 25th percentile and declines further at the 5th percentile. In contrast, Sweden maintains a high position throughout the ability range. The Netherlands has a high average position and improves this for its low achieving pupils. Two other large European countries (France and Germany) tend to show a slight improvement for their lower achieving pupils. Pupils in Italy tend to have an even performance at all of the percentiles.

Figure 2.10 has the same form and shows the data for English-speaking (or testing) countries. This illustrates that the trend shown for England, of a decline in standing across the achievement range, is a fairly general one. Although starting from a lower base, New Zealand and Singapore show the greatest decline; New Zealand being among the top five countries at the 95th percentile but with very low performance at the 5th percentile. Singapore falls from among the top ten countries at the 95th percentile to among the lowest ranked ten at the 5th percentile, but this is perhaps understandable in that the language of instruction and testing is not the home language for the great majority of pupils. The United States and Scotland show the same general pattern. The slight exception is Canada – English only (Ontario and Quebec), for which the decline in the lower percentiles is not as marked. It is interesting to note that when the complete results for Canada, incorporating students tested in both English and French are included, this pattern is not present.

**Figure 2.11   Standardised deviation from average of all countries for England and countries seeking accession to European Union**

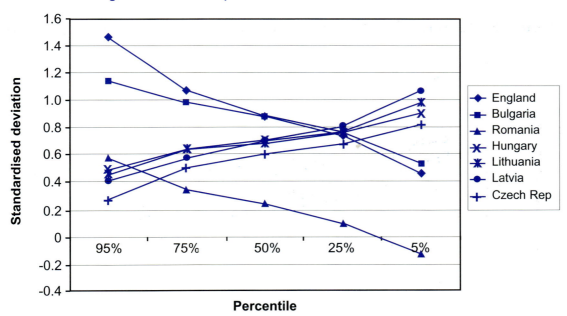

Figure 2.11 shows a similar comparison for the higher scoring countries seeking accession to the European Union: Bulgaria, Latvia, Lithuania, Hungary, and the Czech Republic. Two countries, Bulgaria and Romania, have a pattern similar to that for England, with their most able children scoring highly but a decline in relative performance for their lower achieving pupils. In contrast, the remaining countries (Latvia, Lithuania, Hungary and the Czech Republic) all show a pattern of increasing relative position for their low achieving children.

The reasons for this difference between European countries with lower ranges of attainment and the maintenance of position for their low achieving children, and English-speaking countries with larger ranges of performance and worse performance at the lower percentiles, need further exploration. They may derive from educational factors, such as curriculum and pedagogic practice, or from social factors in the countries related to cohesion or inclusiveness. Finally, they may also derive from the nature of the languages tested. English has many orthographic inconsistencies, and a richness deriving from its many linguistic roots. It is possible that these factors mean it is more difficult for low achieving pupils than more regular languages.

## 2.4    Relationships to other studies

### 1991 IEA Reading Study

England did not formally participate in the previous IEA study of reading, conducted in 1991 (Elley, 1992). However, in 1996 the NFER decided to undertake a partial replication, using a modified version of the tests from the international survey. This covered both England and Wales. These results are presented in an NFER report (Brooks *et al*, 1996) which also details limitations of the study. Some parts of the test showed a ceiling effect which may have reduced the average score. The higher proportion of pupils with special educational needs in mainstream schools in England and Wales and the exclusion from the samples of children repeating a year in those countries employing a grade-based promotion system (such as France and the United States) may have depressed the English and Welsh results in comparison. Finally, the English and Welsh sample were younger than the international average. An adjustment was made for this.

The average score in the IEA test (taken in 1996) would have put England and Wales close to the overall average for the 1991 study, within a group of 13 countries whose average scores were not significantly different. Among these countries were Ireland, Belgium (French-speaking), West Germany, Hungary and The Netherlands. Among countries which had significantly higher scores were Finland, the United States, Sweden, France, Italy, New Zealand and Norway.

Since the nature of the reading tests in 1991 and 2001 was very different, and England and Wales were not part of the survey proper in 1991, any conclusions must be tentative. Nevertheless, there does appear to be a marked increase in the international standing of England from the mid-1990s to PIRLS 2001. England (as with The Netherlands) has moved from a position around the international average to being one of the leading countries in terms of reading achievement. Sweden has notably maintained its high position, but others such as New Zealand and France have a much lower standing in PIRLS than in the 1991 IEA survey.

The reasons for such changes are complex, and can only be judged by a close knowledge of the particular countries concerned, a scrutiny which is beyond this national report for England.

### PISA 2000

The Programme for International Student Assessment (PISA) is a major international study managed by the Organisation for Economic Co-operation and Development (OECD). Its first study was undertaken in 2000 and had as a main focus the reading literacy of 15-year-olds (Gill *et al*, 2002). PISA 2000 included 32 countries, 28 of which are OECD members.

Students in England (and for the United Kingdom as a whole) performed above the OECD average for reading. Only Finland and Canada had significantly higher average scores, and England's students' scores were similar to those of New Zealand, Australia, Ireland, Korea, Japan and Sweden. They were significantly better than those in Norway, Italy, Germany and Switzerland and were markedly above those for the United States.

Since the PIRLS and PISA studies were carried out close together in time, it is tempting to expect similar outcomes. However, the students involved were seven years apart in terms of age and perhaps more importantly, educational experience. Education systems all over the world are changing rapidly, and this is particularly the case in England. The students tested in PISA 2000 would have begun their schooling around the same time as the National Curriculum was being introduced and the impact on them would not have been very great until they were fairly advanced in their school careers. In contrast, the pupils taking part in PIRLS in 2001, at the age of nine, were educated in a system with an established National Curriculum and in their later years, a strong emphasis on literacy. Other countries may or may not have undergone some similar process of change. There is therefore no necessary reason why the PISA and PIRLS results should correspond exactly.

**Figure 2.12    Relationship of PIRLS and PISA**

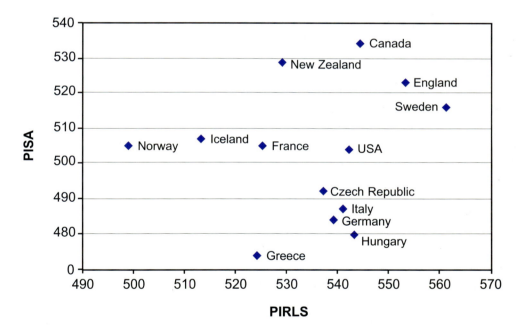

Thirteen countries took part in both PISA and PIRLS, and it is possible to examine the relationships of the two sets of results for literacy. Figure 2.12 shows a scatter plot for the two sets of mean scores for the 15 countries. The correlation between them is 0.15, indicating hardly any association.

A few countries (Sweden, England and Canada) have high scores for both PIRLS and PISA. Others such as Hungary are much higher on PIRLS than PISA, with others, like New Zealand, much higher on PISA than PIRLS. There is no pattern discernible in these relationships, and again the reasons must be sought in individual circumstances.

# 3. Gender Differences in Reading Achievement

---

**The performance of boys and girls at different levels of attainment is looked at in this chapter, along with other evidence about gender differences in reading attainment.**

---

- ■ Girls performed better than boys in all participating countries in PIRLS. In England, girls did particularly well on the literary texts.

- ■ The difference between the scores of boys and girls in England is smaller for the better readers, compared to the difference between boys and girls in the weakest group.

- ■ Girls do better than boys in the national tests in England at the end of key stages 1 and 2. Girls also scored more highly in the PISA study of the reading skills of 15-year-olds in 2000.

## 3.1 Gender differences in PIRLS

In terms of overall achievement, boys in England had the third highest scale score (541), behind those in Sweden and The Netherlands. Girls in England had the second highest scale score (564), exceeded only by Sweden. In common with all other countries participating in PIRLS, the performance of girls was significantly better than that of boys. Table 3.1 shows countries ranked from those with the least difference between the performance of boys and girls to those with the greatest difference.

The difference in the mean achievement of girls and boys in England was 22 scale points, compared to an international difference of 20 scale points. The difference for England was the same as that for Sweden, and greater than that for a number of other European countries including Italy, France, Germany, The Netherlands and Scotland. The difference was less than that for eight countries, including New Zealand and Bulgaria. Table 3.1 also shows that there was no clear relationship between overall achievement and the extent of gender differences. High-achieving countries such as Sweden and England had above average differences between the scale scores of boys and girls, whereas other high achieving countries such as The Netherlands and Canada had below average differences.

## Table 3.1 Average reading achievement by gender

| Countries | Girls | | | Boys | | Achievement Difference |
|---|---|---|---|---|---|---|
| | Per cent | Average Scale Score | | Per cent | Average Scale Score | |
| Italy | 48 (0.9) | 545 (2.6) | ⋏ | 52 (0.9) | 537 (2.7) | 8 (2.5) |
| France | 48 (0.9) | 531 (2.7) | ⋏ | 52 (0.9) | 520 (3.0) | 11 (3.3) |
| Colombia | 50 (1.2) | 428 (5.1) | ⋏ | 50 (1.2) | 416 (4.7) | 12 (4.3) |
| [2a] Russian Federation | 49 (0.9) | 534 (4.3) | ⋏ | 51 (0.9) | 522 (4.8) | 12 (2.3) |
| Czech Republic | 49 (1.0) | 543 (2.8) | ⋏ | 51 (1.0) | 531 (2.6) | 12 (2.8) |
| Germany | 50 (0.8) | 545 (2.2) | ⋏ | 50 (0.8) | 533 (2.5) | 13 (2.7) |
| Romania | 51 (1.0) | 519 (4.2) | ⋏ | 49 (1.0) | 504 (5.7) | 14 (3.8) |
| Hungary | 51 (1.0) | 550 (2.4) | ⋏ | 49 (1.0) | 536 (2.5) | 14 (2.1) |
| [†] Netherlands | 50 (0.8) | 562 (2.7) | ⋏ | 50 (0.8) | 547 (2.8) | 15 (2.2) |
| Slovak Republic | 50 (0.9) | 526 (3.0) | ⋏ | 50 (0.9) | 510 (3.3) | 16 (3.0) |
| [1] Lithuania | 51 (1.0) | 552 (3.0) | ⋏ | 49 (1.0) | 535 (2.7) | 17 (2.7) |
| [†] Scotland | 52 (1.0) | 537 (3.9) | ⋏ | 48 (1.0) | 519 (4.2) | 17 (4.0) |
| [*] [1] Canada (O,Q) | 50 (0.7) | 553 (2.6) | ⋏ | 50 (0.7) | 536 (2.6) | 17 (2.1) |
| [†] United States | 51 (0.8) | 551 (3.8) | ⋏ | 49 (0.8) | 533 (4.9) | 18 (4.1) |
| Argentina | 51 (1.1) | 428 (6.2) | ⋏ | 49 (1.1) | 410 (6.5) | 18 (4.7) |
| Hong Kong, SAR | 50 (1.0) | 538 (3.0) | ⋏ | 50 (1.0) | 519 (3.5) | 19 (2.9) |
| Iceland | 50 (0.8) | 522 (1.9) | ⋏ | 50 (0.8) | 503 (1.5) | 19 (2.4) |
| Turkey | 48 (0.9) | 459 (4.0) | ⋏ | 52 (0.9) | 440 (3.7) | 19 (3.1) |
| International Avg. | 50 (0.2) | 510 (0.7) | ⋏ | 50 (0.2) | 490 (0.7) | 20 (0.7) |
| [‡] Morocco | 45 (1.3) | 361 (9.6) | ⋏ | 55 (1.3) | 341 (10.9) | 20 (6.8) |
| [2a] Greece | 50 (1.0) | 535 (3.8) | ⋏ | 50 (1.0) | 514 (4.0) | 21 (3.9) |
| Macedonia, Rep. of | 49 (0.9) | 452 (5.1) | ⋏ | 51 (0.9) | 431 (4.8) | 21 (3.6) |
| Norway | 48 (1.0) | 510 (3.5) | ⋏ | 52 (1.0) | 489 (3.4) | 21 (3.9) |
| Slovenia | 50 (0.8) | 512 (2.5) | ⋏ | 50 (0.8) | 491 (2.4) | 22 (2.8) |
| Latvia | 48 (1.1) | 556 (3.1) | ⋏ | 52 (1.1) | 534 (2.6) | 22 (3.4) |
| [2b] Israel | 50 (1.3) | 520 (3.4) | ⋏ | 50 (1.3) | 498 (3.7) | 22 (4.3) |
| Sweden | 49 (0.7) | 572 (2.6) | ⋏ | 51 (0.7) | 550 (2.5) | 22 (2.6) |
| [†2a] England | 52 (1.1) | 564 (3.9) | ⋏ | 48 (1.1) | 541 (3.7) | 22 (3.3) |
| Cyprus | 49 (0.9) | 506 (3.3) | ⋏ | 51 (0.9) | 482 (3.6) | 24 (3.5) |
| Bulgaria | 51 (0.9) | 562 (3.7) | ⋏ | 49 (0.9) | 538 (4.7) | 24 (3.6) |
| Singapore | 48 (1.5) | 540 (5.3) | ⋏ | 52 (1.5) | 516 (5.7) | 24 (4.1) |
| Moldova, Rep. of | 50 (1.0) | 504 (4.7) | ⋏ | 50 (1.0) | 479 (4.0) | 25 (4.0) |
| New Zealand | 49 (1.3) | 542 (4.7) | ⋏ | 51 (1.3) | 516 (4.2) | 27 (5.4) |
| Iran, Islamic Rep. of | 55 (3.6) | 426 (5.7) | ⋏ | 45 (3.6) | 399 (5.6) | 27 (8.1) |
| Belize | 50 (0.9) | 341 (5.3) | ⋏ | 50 (0.9) | 314 (5.2) | 27 (4.8) |
| Kuwait        r | 48 (0.3) | 422 (5.6) | ⋏ | 52 (0.3) | 373 (6.3) | 48 (8.4) |
| | | | | | | |
| [*] Quebec (Canada) | 51 (0.9) | 544 (3.4) | ⋏ | 49 (0.9) | 530 (3.1) | 14 (2.7) |
| [*] Ontario (Canada) | 49 (0.9) | 558 (3.8) | ⋏ | 51 (0.9) | 538 (3.4) | 20 (2.7) |

⋏ Significantly higher than other gender

\* Canada is represented by the provinces of Ontario and Quebec only. The international average does not include the results from these provinces separately.
† Met guidelines for sample participation rates only after replacement schools were included.
‡ Nearly satisfying guidelines for sample participation rates after replacement schools were included.
1 National Desired Population does not cover all of International Desired Population. Because coverage falls below 65%, Canada is annotated Canada (O, Q) for the provinces of Ontario and Quebec only.
2a National Defined Population covers less than 95% of National Desired Population.
2b National Defined Population covers less than 80% of National Desired Population.
( ) Standard errors appear in parentheses. Because results are rounded to the nearest whole number, some totals may appear inconsistent.
An "r" indicates data available for 70–84% of the pupils.
Because results are rounded to the nearest whole number, some differences may appear inconsistent.

Source: IEA Progress in International Reading Literacy Study (PIRLS) 2001

Twenty-nine per cent of the girls in the sample in England were in the upper quartile, against 21 per cent of boys. In the lower quartile, the proportions are reversed, with 29 per cent of boys and 21 per cent of girls. This situation in England mirrors the average distribution internationally.

A more detailed comparison of the performance of boys and girls at different points in the achievement distribution is shown in Tables 3.2 and 3.3. These show scale scores for performance at the 5th, 25th, 50th, 75th and 95th percentiles for boys and girls separately for each country. This differs from the data shown in Figure 2.8 and discussed in section 2.3 which uses international benchmarks rather than the distributions for each country.

### Table 3.2   Percentiles of reading achievement (boys)

| Countries | 5th Percentile | 25th Percentile | 50th Percentile | 75th Percentile | 95th Percentile |
|---|---|---|---|---|---|
| Argentina | 252 | 342 | 414 | 478 | 559 |
| Belize | 152 | 237 | 308 | 385 | 492 |
| Bulgaria | 380 | 489 | 548 | 595 | 661 |
| Canada (O,Q) | 408 | 490 | 540 | 585 | 648 |
| Colombia | 282 | 364 | 419 | 472 | 540 |
| Cyprus | 338 | 428 | 489 | 540 | 606 |
| Czech Republic | 413 | 489 | 536 | 578 | 630 |
| England | 384 | 487 | 547 | 602 | 677 |
| France | 392 | 476 | 525 | 569 | 630 |
| Germany | 413 | 490 | 538 | 580 | 632 |
| Greece | 377 | 466 | 519 | 568 | 631 |
| Hong Kong, SAR | 401 | 480 | 524 | 563 | 615 |
| Hungary | 416 | 495 | 540 | 583 | 637 |
| Iceland | 367 | 454 | 508 | 556 | 620 |
| Iran, Islamic Rep. of | 252 | 333 | 398 | 467 | 549 |
| Israel | 320 | 438 | 509 | 566 | 639 |
| Italy | 412 | 491 | 541 | 587 | 648 |
| Kuwait | 223 | 309 | 375 | 441 | 514 |
| Latvia | 431 | 496 | 538 | 575 | 628 |
| Lithuania | 424 | 494 | 539 | 580 | 633 |
| Macedonia, Rep. of | 253 | 355 | 440 | 508 | 585 |
| Moldova, Rep. of | 345 | 430 | 483 | 533 | 599 |
| Morocco | 161 | 259 | 337 | 419 | 533 |
| Netherlands | 449 | 510 | 549 | 587 | 639 |
| New Zealand | 345 | 454 | 527 | 583 | 657 |
| Norway | 337 | 436 | 497 | 548 | 611 |
| Romania | 337 | 448 | 514 | 568 | 643 |
| Russian Federation | 403 | 482 | 527 | 568 | 623 |
| Scotland | 371 | 466 | 526 | 577 | 651 |
| Singapore | 332 | 465 | 530 | 582 | 648 |
| Slovak Republic | 380 | 467 | 516 | 559 | 618 |
| Slovenia | 363 | 444 | 495 | 541 | 603 |
| Sweden | 431 | 510 | 556 | 595 | 652 |
| Turkey | 291 | 382 | 443 | 503 | 577 |
| United States | 372 | 481 | 545 | 596 | 656 |
| International Avg. | 349 | 438 | 495 | 547 | 616 |

Source: IEA Progress in International Reading Literacy Study (PIRLS) 2001

It is clear that the wide range of performance evident for England for the whole sample is reflected in the performance of both boys and girls. For both sexes, pupils at the 75th and 95th percentiles for England have the highest scale scores of all participating countries. At the median, boys have the fourth highest scale score and girls have the third highest. In the case of boys, the scale score is slightly lower than those of Sweden, The Netherlands and Bulgaria. For girls the scale score at the median is slightly lower than those of Sweden and Bulgaria.

At the 25th percentile, both sexes in England tend to be performing less well in relation to other countries. The scale score of 487 for boys at the 25th percentile is exceeded by that of ten other countries. The scale score for girls at the 25th percentile (514) is exceeded by that

**Table 3.3   Percentiles of reading achievement (girls)**

| Countries | 5th Percentile | 25th Percentile | 50th Percentile | 75th Percentile | 95th Percentile |
|---|---|---|---|---|---|
| Argentina | 262 | 364 | 433 | 495 | 577 |
| Belize | 173 | 266 | 337 | 413 | 522 |
| Bulgaria | 423 | 514 | 570 | 616 | 681 |
| Canada (O,Q) | 430 | 507 | 554 | 602 | 667 |
| Colombia | 293 | 372 | 429 | 486 | 560 |
| Cyprus | 370 | 455 | 510 | 561 | 626 |
| Czech Republic | 434 | 505 | 547 | 586 | 638 |
| England | 411 | 514 | 569 | 621 | 692 |
| France | 413 | 487 | 531 | 577 | 641 |
| Germany | 425 | 504 | 550 | 592 | 647 |
| Greece | 419 | 487 | 538 | 583 | 641 |
| Hong Kong, SAR | 434 | 501 | 541 | 578 | 628 |
| Hungary | 441 | 510 | 554 | 594 | 648 |
| Iceland | 397 | 477 | 525 | 571 | 635 |
| Iran, Islamic Rep. of | 269 | 363 | 429 | 493 | 567 |
| Israel | 355 | 462 | 531 | 583 | 652 |
| Italy | 418 | 503 | 551 | 593 | 650 |
| Kuwait | 282 | 366 | 425 | 478 | 551 |
| Latvia | 450 | 516 | 560 | 598 | 648 |
| Lithuania | 442 | 511 | 555 | 597 | 648 |
| Macedonia, Rep. of | 273 | 379 | 463 | 529 | 602 |
| Moldova, Rep. of | 383 | 458 | 506 | 553 | 615 |
| Morocco | 178 | 279 | 361 | 439 | 548 |
| Netherlands | 469 | 525 | 563 | 599 | 651 |
| New Zealand | 379 | 487 | 550 | 604 | 679 |
| Norway | 367 | 466 | 517 | 562 | 626 |
| Romania | 366 | 465 | 525 | 579 | 651 |
| Russian Federation | 421 | 494 | 539 | 578 | 631 |
| Scotland | 384 | 485 | 541 | 593 | 664 |
| Singapore | 373 | 493 | 550 | 601 | 666 |
| Slovak Republic | 404 | 488 | 532 | 571 | 627 |
| Slovenia | 391 | 470 | 517 | 559 | 617 |
| Sweden | 463 | 534 | 575 | 614 | 672 |
| Turkey | 316 | 404 | 461 | 518 | 593 |
| United States | 414 | 502 | 558 | 605 | 672 |
| International Avg. | 375 | 460 | 514 | 563 | 630 |

Source: IEA Progress in International Reading Literacy Study (PIRLS) 2001

of three countries. For pupils who are at the 5th percentile in their country's distribution, the performance of boys in England was surpassed by that of boys in 12 other countries, and also by 15 countries for girls.

The difference between the scale scores of boys and girls at different points in the distribution is shown in Table 3.4. In this table, countries are ranked by overall performance (as in Figure 2.1). In all countries, girls scored higher than boys at each point in the distribution. In the majority of countries the difference in the performance of boys and girls was greater at the 5th than at the 95th percentile. In England, the scale score of boys at the 95th percentile was 15 scale points lower than that of girls and at the 5th percentile it was 27 scale points lower, differences which were broadly in line with the international average.

## 3.2     Gender differences in reading for different purposes

The performance of boys and girls in reading for the two different purposes identified in the PIRLS assessments is detailed in Table 3.5. In the majority of countries, including England, the gender difference was greater in reading for literary purposes than in reading for informational purposes. In England the average difference between the scores of boys and girls when reading for literary purposes was particularly high at 30 scale points. In reading for information purposes, the difference was less at 17 points and close to the international average.

On the literary scale, both boys and girls in England have the highest scale scores at the 75th and 95th percentiles of all participating countries. At the median, boys in England had the third highest scale score and girls the highest. At the lower end of the distribution, the spread of achievement in England is apparent with boys in nine countries scoring more highly at the 25th percentile and girls in two countries.

On the information scales, both boys and girls in England were amongst the three highest scoring countries at both the 75th and 95th percentiles. At the median, boys and girls had the fourth and fifth highest scale scores respectively. For pupils at the 25th percentile, the score of boys was exceeded by boys in 11 countries and that of girls by girls in six countries.

## 3.3     Other evidence of gender differences in reading achievement

In the reading element of the PISA study in 2000, girls achieved significantly higher results than boys in all countries and on all three component scales. In contrast to PIRLS, however, the difference between the mean scale scores of boys and girls in England was less than the international average. There was no relationship between the extent of gender differences and achievement. The difference between the performance of boys and girls in England increased as achievement fell, in line with what was observed in PIRLS. In PISA, the difference between the highest attaining boys and girls (those at the 95th percentile) was 11 scale points whereas between boys and girls at the 5th percentile it was 38 scale points.

Table 3.4   Difference in scale scores for boys and girls

| Countries | 5th Percentile | 25th Percentile | 50th Percentile | 75th Percentile | 95th Percentile |
|---|---|---|---|---|---|
| Sweden | 32 | 24 | 19 | 19 | 20 |
| Netherlands | 20 | 15 | 14 | 12 | 12 |
| England | 27 | 27 | 22 | 19 | 15 |
| Bulgaria | 43 | 25 | 22 | 21 | 20 |
| Latvia | 19 | 20 | 22 | 23 | 20 |
| Canada (O,Q) | 22 | 17 | 14 | 17 | 19 |
| Lithuania | 18 | 17 | 16 | 17 | 15 |
| Hungary | 25 | 15 | 14 | 11 | 11 |
| United States | 42 | 21 | 13 | 9 | 16 |
| Italy | 6 | 12 | 10 | 6 | 2 |
| Germany | 12 | 14 | 12 | 12 | 15 |
| Czech Republic | 21 | 16 | 11 | 8 | 8 |
| New Zealand | 34 | 33 | 23 | 21 | 22 |
| Scotland | 13 | 19 | 15 | 16 | 13 |
| Singapore | 41 | 28 | 20 | 19 | 18 |
| Russian Federation | 18 | 12 | 12 | 10 | 8 |
| Hong Kong, SAR | 33 | 21 | 17 | 15 | 13 |
| France | 21 | 11 | 6 | 8 | 11 |
| Greece | 42 | 21 | 19 | 15 | 10 |
| Slovak Republic | 24 | 21 | 16 | 12 | 9 |
| Iceland | 30 | 23 | 17 | 15 | 15 |
| Romania | 29 | 17 | 11 | 11 | 8 |
| Israel | 35 | 24 | 22 | 17 | 13 |
| Slovenia | 28 | 26 | 22 | 18 | 14 |
| Norway | 30 | 30 | 20 | 14 | 15 |
| Cyprus | 32 | 27 | 21 | 21 | 20 |
| Moldova, Rep. of | 38 | 28 | 23 | 20 | 16 |
| Turkey | 25 | 22 | 18 | 15 | 16 |
| Macedonia, Rep. of | 20 | 24 | 23 | 21 | 17 |
| Colombia | 11 | 8 | 10 | 14 | 20 |
| Argentina | 10 | 22 | 19 | 17 | 18 |
| Iran, Islamic Rep. of | 17 | 30 | 31 | 26 | 18 |
| Kuwait | 59 | 57 | 50 | 37 | 37 |
| Morocco | 17 | 20 | 24 | 20 | 15 |
| Belize | 21 | 29 | 29 | 28 | 30 |
| International Avg. | 26 | 22 | 19 | 17 | 16 |

Source: IEA Progress in International Reading Literacy Study (PIRLS) 2001

## Table 3.5  Reading for literary and informational purposes by gender

| Countries | Literary | | | Informational | | |
|---|---|---|---|---|---|---|
| | Girls Average Scale Score | Boys Average Scale Score | Difference | Girls Average Scale Score | Boys Average Scale Score | Difference |
| Argentina | 429 (6.2) ⌃ | 408 (6.2) | 21 (4.6) | 429 (6.0) ⌃ | 415 (5.9) | 15 (4.9) |
| Belize | 340 (5.3) ⌃ | 320 (5.6) | 20 (5.1) | 349 (5.1) ⌃ | 316 (5.9) | 32 (5.0) |
| Bulgaria | 563 (4.2) ⌃ | 535 (5.1) | 28 (5.4) | 561 (3.4) ⌃ | 541 (4.2) | 20 (3.1) |
| *[1] Canada (O,Q) | 554 (3.0) ⌃ | 535 (2.7) | 19 (2.2) | 549 (3.0) ⌃ | 534 (2.6) | 16 (2.7) |
| Colombia | 431 (4.9) ⌃ | 419 (4.8) | 12 (4.6) | 430 (5.2) ⌃ | 417 (4.9) | 12 (5.4) |
| Cyprus | 512 (2.9) ⌃ | 485 (3.3) | 26 (3.7) | 500 (3.1) ⌃ | 480 (3.5) | 20 (2.8) |
| Czech Republic | 543 (2.7) ⌃ | 528 (2.7) | 14 (2.8) | 541 (3.3) ⌃ | 532 (3.1) | 9 (3.5) |
| †2a England | 574 (4.9) ⌃ | 544 (4.0) | 30 (4.3) | 554 (4.0) ⌃ | 537 (4.0) | 17 (3.5) |
| France | 524 (2.9) ⌃ | 513 (3.2) | 11 (3.2) | 540 (2.9) ⌃ | 527 (3.1) | 12 (3.3) |
| Germany | 544 (2.1) ⌃ | 529 (2.4) | 14 (2.5) | 543 (2.5) ⌃ | 533 (2.1) | 10 (2.6) |
| 2a Greece | 539 (3.8) ⌃ | 516 (3.7) | 23 (3.5) | 529 (3.9) ⌃ | 513 (4.4) | 15 (3.8) |
| Hong Kong, SAR | 528 (3.4) ⌃ | 507 (3.4) | 21 (3.4) | 546 (2.8) ⌃ | 529 (3.6) | 17 (3.1) |
| Hungary | 558 (2.1) ⌃ | 538 (2.6) | 20 (2.5) | 542 (2.5) ⌃ | 532 (2.8) | 10 (3.0) |
| Iceland | 531 (1.9) ⌃ | 509 (1.7) | 21 (2.4) | 512 (1.9) ⌃ | 496 (2.0) | 16 (2.6) |
| Iran, Islamic Rep. of | 433 (5.7) ⌃ | 406 (6.4) | 28 (8.7) | 419 (6.4) ⌃ | 395 (6.1) | 24 (8.8) |
| 2b Israel | 521 (3.3) ⌃ | 498 (3.2) | 23 (3.9) | 518 (3.5) ⌃ | 495 (3.6) | 23 (4.2) |
| Italy | 549 (2.7) ⌃ | 538 (3.3) | 11 (2.8) | 539 (2.7) ⌃ | 533 (2.6) | 6 (2.6) |
| Kuwait | 416 (5.2) ⌃ | 373 (5.4) | 43 (7.4) | 430 (6.1) ⌃ | 378 (6.7) | 52 (9.1) |
| Latvia | 548 (2.8) ⌃ | 527 (2.2) | 21 (2.4) | 558 (2.8) ⌃ | 537 (2.6) | 22 (2.8) |
| 1 Lithuania | 554 (3.4) ⌃ | 536 (3.7) | 18 (3.8) | 548 (2.9) ⌃ | 532 (2.9) | 16 (2.8) |
| Macedonia, Rep. of | 453 (4.6) ⌃ | 430 (4.9) | 22 (3.3) | 454 (5.6) ⌃ | 437 (5.8) | 17 (4.8) |
| Moldova, Rep. of | 492 (4.3) ⌃ | 468 (3.6) | 23 (3.4) | 516 (5.5) ⌃ | 494 (4.7) | 23 (4.5) |
| ‡ Morocco | 358 (8.5) ⌃ | 340 (9.1) | 19 (5.1) | 370 (10.8) ⌃ | 349 (11.9) | 20 (6.3) |
| † Netherlands | 561 (2.8) ⌃ | 544 (3.2) | 17 (3.3) | 559 (2.9) ⌃ | 547 (2.9) | 11 (2.4) |
| New Zealand | 546 (4.7) ⌃ | 517 (4.6) | 30 (5.1) | 536 (4.5) ⌃ | 514 (4.4) | 21 (4.6) |
| Norway | 519 (3.4) ⌃ | 494 (3.1) | 24 (3.6) | 499 (3.7) ⌃ | 486 (3.1) | 14 (3.9) |
| Romania | 518 (4.2) ⌃ | 505 (6.1) | 13 (4.4) | 519 (4.6) ⌃ | 506 (5.6) | 13 (4.3) |
| 2a Russian Federation | 531 (3.9) ⌃ | 517 (4.3) | 14 (2.9) | 536 (4.5) ⌃ | 527 (4.6) | 9 (2.8) |
| † Scotland | 538 (4.0) ⌃ | 519 (4.1) | 19 (3.9) | 534 (4.3) ⌃ | 520 (4.1) | 14 (4.4) |
| Singapore | 541 (5.7) ⌃ | 516 (6.0) | 25 (4.2) | 538 (4.9) ⌃ | 517 (5.3) | 21 (3.8) |
| Slovak Republic | 519 (2.9) ⌃ | 505 (2.9) | 14 (2.8) | 530 (2.8) ⌃ | 514 (3.4) | 16 (3.3) |
| Slovenia | 509 (2.4) ⌃ | 490 (2.4) | 19 (3.1) | 514 (2.6) ⌃ | 492 (2.5) | 21 (3.4) |
| Sweden | 572 (2.9) ⌃ | 547 (2.6) | 25 (2.8) | 568 (2.8) ⌃ | 550 (2.6) | 18 (3.2) |
| Turkey | 460 (3.8) ⌃ | 437 (3.6) | 22 (2.9) | 460 (4.6) ⌃ | 444 (4.2) | 16 (4.5) |
| † United States | 558 (4.2) ⌃ | 542 (4.6) | 16 (4.3) | 541 (4.1) ⌃ | 525 (4.3) | 16 (4.0) |
| International Avg. | 511 (0.7) ⌃ | 490 (0.7) | 21 (0.7) | 509 (0.7) ⌃ | 491 (0.8) | 18 (0.8) |
| * Ontario (Canada) | 563 (4.0) ⌃ | 540 (3.3) | 24 (3.2) | 550 (3.9) ⌃ | 533 (3.4) | 17 (3.5) |
| * Quebec (Canada) | 541 (3.5) ⌃ | 526 (3.4) | 15 (3.5) | 546 (3.3) ⌃ | 535 (3.1) | 10 (2.9) |

⌃ Significantly higher than other gender

\* Canada is represented by the provinces of Ontario and Quebec only. The international average does not include the results from these provinces separately.
† Met guidelines for sample participation rates only after replacement schools were included.
‡ Nearly satisfying guidelines for sample participation rates after replacement schools were included.
1 National Desired Population does not cover all of International Desired Population. Because coverage falls below 65%, Canada is annotated Canada (O, Q) for the provinces of Ontario and Quebec only.
2a National Defined Population covers less than 95% of National Desired Population.
2b National Defined Population covers less than 80% of National Desired Population.
( ) Standard errors appear in parentheses.
Because results are rounded to the nearest whole number, some differences may appear inconsistent.

Source: IEA Progress in International Reading Literacy Study (PIRLS) 2001

There is repeated evidence from the statutory tests of reading in England at key stages 1 and 2 of girls outperforming boys.  At key stage 1 in 2002, 80 per cent of boys and 88 per cent of girls achieved level 2 or above, while 26 per cent of boys and 34 per cent of girls achieved level 3.  At key stage 2 in 2002 a similar pattern emerged.  With the older group, 77 per cent of boys and 83 per cent of girls achieved level 4 or above, with 35 per cent of boys and 41 per cent of girls achieving level 5, above the expected level.

The distribution of marks on the 2002 key stage 2 reading test was analysed for the pupils in the PIRLS sample for England.  This revealed that 26 per cent of girls and 22 per cent of boys were in the upper quartile, and 23 per cent of girls and 27 per cent of boys were in the lower quartile, a slightly more balanced distribution than was found in the PIRLS reading assessment.

# 4.  The PIRLS Reading Literacy Tests

The PIRLS survey produced findings that compared the reading literacy performance of children in different countries.  However, 'reading literacy' can be defined in many different ways – from the simple pronunciation of written words to the ability to understand and use complex information – so it is important to clarify what skills and understandings are involved for children of this age.  This chapter will examine the PIRLS framework and tests to illustrate the kinds of reading skills demonstrated by children in this survey, and relate this information to the National Curriculum in England.

- ■ PIRLS adopts this definition of reading literacy:

  *The ability to understand and use those written language forms required by society and/or valued by the individual.  Young readers can construct meaning from a variety of texts.  They read to learn, to participate in communities of readers, and for enjoyment.*

- ■ The assessment includes different types of reading passage.  Half of them are stories, and the other half give factual information.

- ■ The top ten per cent of children showed a complete understanding of what they had read, bringing together ideas and forming opinions based on the text.  Those in the lowest band of performance could select the right answer to a simple question.  Some examples of questions and answers are given in this chapter.

- ■ Children in England following the National Curriculum were well prepared for the demands of the PIRLS test.  The National Curriculum, too, requires both literature and factual reading.  Children are taught to use inference, to formulate opinions and to analyse what they have read.

- ■ The PIRLS children went on to take their national key stage 2 tests a year later, in 2002.  Some of the questions in this test are similar to those in PIRLS and a few are more demanding than anything in PIRLS.

## 4.1    Reading literacy in PIRLS

The development of the PIRLS tests was preceded by the creation of a reading framework by a group of international specialists (Campbell *et al, 2001*). The definition of reading and the specifications for the test were outlined in this framework, underpinning the subsequent test development. The framework was reviewed, revised and finally accepted by all the participating countries before the tests were developed.

The PIRLS framework recognises the particular features of developing readers at the age of 9–10 years, and gives the following definition of reading literacy:

> *The ability to understand and use those written language forms required by society and/or valued by the individual. Young readers can construct meaning from a variety of texts. They read to learn, to participate in communities of readers, and for enjoyment.*

This presents a view of reading literacy as a complex interactive activity, in accordance with recent research. It acknowledges that children of this age read mainly at home and at school, rather than as a means of participating directly in the adult world. Enjoyment of reading is central, but these children also need increasingly to understand written material in order to learn across the curriculum. For these diverse purposes, they can understand and use a range of text types.

The definition of reading leads into the basic structure of the PIRLS assessment. Firstly, two overarching purposes for reading are distinguished:

- reading for literary experience

- reading to acquire and use information.

In literary reading, the reader becomes involved in imagined events, setting, actions, consequences, characters, atmosphere, feelings, and ideas, bringing his or her own experiences, feeling, appreciation of language, and knowledge of literary forms to the text. In reading for information, the reader engages not with imagined worlds, but with aspects of the real universe. Through informational texts, one can understand how the world is and has been, and why things work as they do. These texts take many forms, but one major distinction is between chronological and non-chronological organisations.

Each of these purposes for reading is often associated with certain types of texts. For example, reading for literary experience is often accomplished through reading fiction, while reading to acquire and use information is generally associated with informative articles and instructional texts. The early reading of most young children centres on literary and narrative text types. In addition, many young readers also enjoy acquiring information from books and other types of reading material. This kind of reading becomes more important as pupils develop their literacy abilities and are increasingly required to read in order to learn across the curriculum.

These purposes inform the selection of passages for pupils to read. Half of them are stories that fulfil the literary purpose, and the other half non-fiction texts of various kinds that relate to the informational purpose.

The other dimension of the PIRLS structure is a set of four reading processes, which determine the kinds of questions that are asked about each text. These are:

- focus on and retrieve explicitly stated information

- make straightforward inferences

- interpret and integrate ideas and information

- examine and evaluate content, language and textual elements.

The diagram in Figure 4.1 illustrates this structure, and also lists the percentages of the PIRLS tests devoted to each element. The discussion of pupil performance below will give examples of questions and expand upon the kinds of answers that children were able to supply.

**Figure 4.1   Structure of the PIRLS assessment**

|  | Purposes for reading | | |
|---|---|---|---|
| **Processes of comprehension** | Literary experience | Acquire and use information | |
| Focus on and retrieve explicitly stated information | | | 20% |
| Make straightforward inferences | | | 30% |
| Interpret and integrate ideas and information | | | 30% |
| Examine and evaluate content, language and textual elements | | | 20% |
|  | 50% | 50% | |

In accordance with the framework, the texts used in the PIRLS assessment are all full-length stories or information pieces – 400–700 words – containing sufficient depth and interest to give rise to questions covering all four processes. Pupils' responses as they make inferences or integrate and evaluate ideas cannot be captured fully by multiple-choice questions, and within the PIRLS tests about half of the marks are awarded for expressing understanding in writing in an open response format.

The tests were developed over a two-year period from 1999 to 2001 (Sainsbury and Campbell, 2002). The aim, in this international context, was to produce tests that were accessible in their content and style to children in all the participating countries, and that respected the diverse cultural traditions and the reading literacy curriculum of the pupils. In order to achieve this, the test development process included repeated reviews by the international specialist group that had devised the framework – the Reading Development Group – and by representatives of all the participating countries. The passages were international in origin, derived from a search involving contributions from 14 countries, and the questions were reviewed and revised at a series of international meetings. At the end of the initial development process, there were 16 blocks in existence – twice as many as needed

– from which a final selection had to be made. In autumn 2000, 30 countries undertook field trials of all this material, and the final choice of blocks was agreed at a further international meeting. The result was a PIRLS assessment with a unique, genuinely international character, consistent with but different from reading tests in any of the individual countries.

This final assessment comprised eight 'blocks', each consisting of text and questions, which were administered in a matrix sampling design as described in Chapter 1, so that each pupil took only two of them. Four of the blocks were literary texts and four of them informational. The examples in this chapter are drawn from the two literary and two informational blocks that have been released to the public, which are described in Figure 4.2. These four blocks represent only half of the assessment – the others remain confidential – but give a clear idea of the variety of texts and questions included.

**Figure 4.2   Description of four test blocks**

| Text | Purpose | Description |
| --- | --- | --- |
| *Hare Heralds the Earthquake*<br><br>Rosalind Kerven | Literary experience | A tale in traditional style with animal characters. Hare panics as he mistakes the crash of a fruit falling for an earthquake; the wiser lion shows him his mistake.<br><br>Eleven questions, five multiple choice and six open response. |
| *Nights of the Pufflings*<br><br>Bruce McMillan | Use and acquire information | An information text from Iceland explaining how pufflings (baby puffins) are helped to find their way back to sea each year by the children of the island.<br><br>Thirteen questions, eight multiple choice and five open response. |
| These two texts were presented together in a full colour booklet entitled *The Natural World*. | | |
| *The Upside-Down Mice*<br><br>Roald Dahl | Literary experience | A quirky tale in which an old man rids his house of mice by means of a complicated trick which involves sticking all the furniture to the ceiling.<br><br>Fourteen questions, seven multiple choice and seven open response. |
| *River Trail* | Use and acquire information | A leaflet which combines a description of a bike trail along a river with information about bike hire; both informative and persuasive in purpose.<br><br>Eleven questions, three multiple choice, five open response and three questions in other closed formats. |

The other four texts broadened the range and included contemporary fiction, biography, information with diagrams and a letter.

The marking of multiple choice and other closed questions was straightforward. However, in marking open response questions, mark schemes were needed that allowed children to express their responses in different ways. These mark schemes were developed using pupils' responses from trials. For each open response question, the mark scheme consisted of criteria, evidence and examples. Some of these questions had only one mark, but in others, a full response obtained two or three marks, while partial credit was given for less full answers. Marker training involved representatives from all the participating countries in lengthy discussion of example answers.

## 4.2    Children's performance in PIRLS

Children in England performed very well for both reading purposes, literary and informational. However, their achievements when reading for literary experience were rather higher than when reading to acquire and use information. England was placed joint top of the table for literary reading, but in fifth place for reading to acquire and use information. Chapter 2 gives further details of this.

In order to aid interpretation of the results, the PIRLS analysis included a process known as scale anchoring. This gives descriptions of the reading literacy skills of pupils related to different scores on the assessment, known as international benchmarks. The benchmark descriptions are based on percentile performance. That is, all the pupils in the survey are placed in rank order according to their scores. Those above the 90th percentile scored better than 90 per cent of the international sample, so are in the top ten per cent of performance internationally. Similarly, those at the 50th percentile represent performance in the middle of the range. By selecting test questions that were answered successfully by pupils at each of these benchmarks, it is possible to describe in detail the reading literacy skills and understandings that these children can demonstrate.

### Performance at the 90th percentile

At this, the highest level of performance, England came top of the international table, with a larger proportion of very high achievers, 24 per cent, than any other country. The scale anchoring analysis makes it possible to describe what these children can do.

In reading for literary experience, the top 10 per cent international benchmark description is as follows:

Given short stories with one or two episodes of problem/resolution and essentially two central characters, students can:

- integrate ideas across a text to provide interpretations of a character's traits, intentions and feelings, and give text-based support

- integrate ideas across the text to explain the broader significance or theme of the story.

Figure 4.3, a question from *Hare Heralds the Earthquake*, shows how the PIRLS assessment requires children to bring together ideas: in this case to consider the contrast between the characters of the hare and the lion. There are three marks available for a fully developed response which not only describes the difference between the two characters, but also identifies some evidence for this in the form of the characters' actions. Children in this top-performing group could provide an extensive answer of this kind.

**Figure 4.3   A question from *Hare Heralds the Earthquake***

**Purpose: reading for literary experience**

**Process: interpret and integrate ideas and information**

10.   You learn what the lion and the hare are like from the things they do in the story. Describe how the lion and the hare are different from each other and what each does that shows this.

*The hare is really worried and foolish and the lion is smart and not afraid of a lot of things. The lion showed him what the earthquake was the hare ran away from the fake "earthquake".*

| England: 20% | International average: 14% |
|---|---|

This was a difficult question, with only 14 per cent of children internationally gaining all three marks.  In England, the proportion was 20 per cent.

The next example, from *The Upside-Down Mice*, demonstrates how children at this benchmark can take an overview of the broader significance of events in the story (see Figure 4.4).  Although this is only a one-mark question, it tests whether pupils have grasped that the old man, Labon, had his trick in mind throughout the complicated course of events in the story.  Fifty-one per cent of children in England succeeded on this question, against an international average of 31 per cent.

**Figure 4.4   A question from *The Upside-Down Mice***

**Purpose: reading for literary experience**

**Process: interpret and integrate ideas and information**

4.   Why did Labon smile when he saw there were no mice in the traps?

*Labon knew that the mice did not know his trick yet.*

| England: 51% | International average: 31% |
|---|---|

In reading to acquire and use information, the top 10 per cent benchmark description is:

> Given a variety of short informational materials including text, maps, illustrations, diagrams and photographs organised topically or chronologically, students can:
>
> - integrate information from various texts and their own knowledge, and apply it to situations that might be encountered in the real world.

Figure 4.5, from *Nights of the Pufflings*, illustrates this ability to apply ideas from the text to real-life experience. The text explains that the pufflings are thought to land in the village, rather than on the sea, because the village lights are confused with reflected moonlight. Children giving correct answers are able to apply this new knowledge to their existing understanding, and explain how the situation would be different by daylight.

**Figure 4.5  A question from *Nights of the Pufflings***

| Purpose: reading to acquire and use information |
| --- |
| Process: make straightforward inferences |

10. Why does it need to be daylight when the children release the pufflings? Use information from the article to explain.

*It has to be daylight so that the pufflings don't get confused again by the lights in the village.*

| England: 29% | International average: 25% |
| --- | --- |

Similarly, the next example (Figure 4.6) shows how children at this benchmark can make use of the information in the *River Trail* leaflet and apply it to a hypothetical real-life situation that they are given. The question is about a family with two adults and two children who are 10 years old and 3 years old. They are planning to spend a day cycling along the River Trail.

**Figure 4.6  A question from *River Trail***

| Purpose: reading to acquire and use information |
| --- |
| Process: interpret and integrate ideas and information |

8. Which bikes would the family need? Use what you have read in the leaflet to answer.

*They would need a child seat attached to another bike and a tandem.*

| England: 39% | International average: 26% |
| --- | --- |

England's performance on all four of these example questions was significantly better than the international average at the top 10 per cent benchmark.

nfer

## Median performance

The next set of examples will illustrate the reading skills and understandings of children at the median benchmark, in the middle of the range of performance. England had 72 per cent of the sample achieving at or above this benchmark, again a significantly better standard than the international average. Three other countries had better performance than England at this benchmark. The following is a description of this performance.

Given short stories with one or two episodes of problem/resolution and essentially two central characters, students can:

- recognise and state relationships between events (eg, why something happened) by inferring connections among clearly related sentences

- recognise the overall message or effect of the story

- identify elements of story structure including plot and character (eg, narrator, role of major character, sequence of events, beginning/end)

- make elementary interpretations of a character's actions and aims, drawing on different parts of the text.

Given a variety of short informational materials including text, maps, illustrations, diagrams and photographs organised topically or chronologically, students can:

- make inferences to locate and extract or match explicitly stated information from text

- locate the appropriate section of a leaflet containing text, tables, a map and pictures, and extract some relevant information

- give a general reaction to the whole text, sometimes supported by a specific example.

The following two examples, one from *Hare Heralds the Earthquake* (Figure 4.7) and the second from *Nights of the Pufflings* (Figure 4.8), illustrate the qualities of these answers. These children have a good basic understanding of what they have read, but are less able to integrate ideas and draw upon their own experiences to enhance their understanding of the text.

**Figure 4.7   A question from *Hare Heralds the Earthquake***

| Purpose: reading for literary experience |
| --- |
| Process: interpret and integrate ideas and information |

8.  Do you think the lion liked the hare? What happens in the story that shows this?

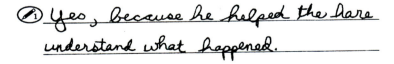

① Yes, because he helped the hare understand what happened.

| England: 71% | International average: 51% |
| --- | --- |

This question, when compared with Figure 4.3, demonstrates the difference between the ability of the highest performers, who can integrate several ideas and explain relationships, and the ability of these middle-band pupils, who are able to make an inference about the feelings of the lion and support it with an example, a less complex demand than contrasting two characters.

**Figure 4.8  A question from *Nights of the Pufflings***

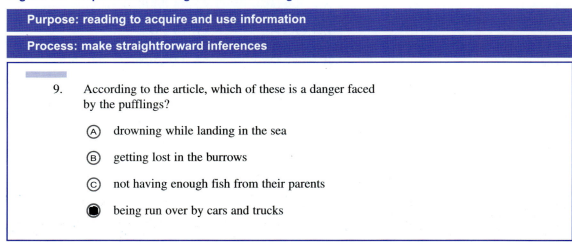

| **Purpose: reading to acquire and use information** |
| **Process: make straightforward inferences** |

9.    According to the article, which of these is a danger faced by the pufflings?

     (A)    drowning while landing in the sea

     (B)    getting lost in the burrows

     (C)    not having enough fish from their parents

     ●    being run over by cars and trucks

| England: 76% | International average: 71% |

In this example, the multiple choice format offers four plausible alternatives, and a sound understanding of the text is needed to locate the information corresponding to the correct response.

For both of these questions, children in England scored significantly better than the international average.

## Performance at the 25th percentile

Performance at this benchmark was consistent with England's overall high position in the international tables and, just as at the 90th and 50th percentiles, the proportion of children reaching or exceeding this standard was above the international average, at 90 per cent. However, the spread of achievement in the England sample was very clear here, as there was a comparatively high proportion of low achievers. There were 12 countries where the lowest group performed better than in England, with over 90 per cent reaching or exceeding this benchmark.

Pupils' reading literacy skills at this benchmark are characterised as follows.

Given short stories with one or two episodes of problem/resolution and essentially two central characters, students can:

● retrieve and reproduce explicitly stated details about a character's actions and feelings presented through narration, description or dialogue

● locate the relevant part of the story and use it to make inferences clearly suggested by the text.

*nfer*

Given a variety of short informational materials including text, maps, illustrations, diagrams and photographs organised topically or chronologically, students can:

● locate and reproduce explicitly stated facts about people, places and animals

● locate the sentence with relevant information and use it to make inferences clearly suggested by the text.

At this benchmark, therefore, children can access the text and form a basic impression of its content, but their understanding tends to be confined to what is literally stated, rather than making inferences or drawing together information from different parts of the text. The following examples, one from each of the four texts (Figures 4.9–4.12), demonstrate the less developed quality of this understanding.

**Figure 4.9   A question from *Hare Heralds the Earthquake***

**Purpose: reading for literary experience**

**Process: focus on and retrieve explicitly stated information and ideas**

2.   What made the whole earth shake?

    Ⓐ   an earthquake

    🔘   an enormous fruit

    ©   the fleeing hares

    Ⓓ   a falling tree

England: 91%                                     International average: 86%

**Figure 4.10   A question from *The Upside-Down Mice***

**Purpose: reading for literary experience**

**Process: focus on and retrieve explicitly stated information and ideas**

10.   Where did Labon put the mice when he picked them up from the floor?

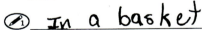

England: 91%                                     International average: 84%

**Figure 4.11   A question from *Nights of the Pufflings***

| Purpose: reading to acquire and use information | *nfer* |
|---|---|

**Process: focus on and retrieve explicitly stated information and ideas**

3.   Why do the puffins come to the island?

   Ⓐ   to be rescued

   Ⓑ   to look for food

   ⬤   to lay eggs

   Ⓓ   to learn to fly

| England: 88% | International average: 78% |
|---|---|

**Figure 4.12   A question from *River Trail***

**Purpose: reading to acquire and use information**

**Process: focus on and retrieve explicitly stated information and ideas**

3.   Where does the River Trail start?

   Ⓐ   Banheim

   Ⓑ   Gründorf

   ⬤   Altenberg

   Ⓓ   Riverside Valley Park

| England: 90% | International average: 82% |
|---|---|

All four of Figures 4.9 to 4.12 are questions that require children to locate a piece of information explicitly stated in the text and simply to reproduce it, without drawing any conclusions or moving beyond what is stated. It is also noteworthy that the multiple choice format provides support in three of the four examples, by offering children options from which to select, rather than asking them to construct their own written response.

Overall, these were easy questions for the international sample, but once again all of them were answered by children in England significantly better than the international average.

## 4.3    PIRLS and the National Curriculum

The children participating in the PIRLS study in England can be expected to have been taught reading literacy in accordance with the programmes of study of the National Curriculum. In most cases, teaching will also have reflected the national literacy strategy (NLS) framework for teaching. This strategy, a detailed structure for teaching the National Curriculum, was introduced during the autumn term of 1998, so the children participating in the 2001 PIRLS survey may have been taught according to its objectives for more than two-and-a half of their five years of compulsory schooling. In Chapter 6, questionnaire responses from headteachers and teachers are reported, and these give further details of the reading curriculum actually experienced by the children in the sample.

The programme of study for reading at key stage 2 requires breadth of study including literature, on the one hand, and non-fiction and non-literary texts, on the other. This division is very close to the PIRLS distinction between reading for literary experience and reading to acquire and use information. The NLS framework for teaching defines a range of both literary and non-fiction text types. For example, for year 5, the age group in which the PIRLS survey was carried out, the framework includes novels, poetry, playscripts, traditional stories, fables, myths, legends, recounts, instructions, non-chronological reports and explanations.

In terms of the types of reading material expected for children of this age, therefore, there is a close match between the curriculum that year 5 pupils have been following and the types of text used in PIRLS. The range in PIRLS is narrower than that of the National Curriculum. In an international survey, with translated texts, it was decided not to include poetry. Playscripts, instructions and numerous other text types expected under the National Curriculum do not appear in this PIRLS assessment.

The National Curriculum also sets out the knowledge, skills and understanding that children need to acquire in the course of key stage 2. This includes a range of strategies for understanding texts, acquiring, using and evaluating information, appreciating literature and learning about language structure and variation. This range of strategies is worked out in more detail in the termly objectives of the NLS framework for teaching. Pupils are systematically introduced to the features of different types of texts and taught to understand, evaluate and produce them.

The National Curriculum reading tests in England are now structured according to a set of reading assessment focuses that can be mapped on to the PIRLS processes as set out in Figure 4.13.

As Figure 4.13 shows, the National Curriculum introduces more differentiation within the broad area encompassed within the fourth PIRLS category. This reflects the fact that the assessment focuses cover all three key stages in England, relating to pupils up to 14 years of age, rather than the narrower group of 9–10 year olds in PIRLS. Conversely, there is greater differentiation within PIRLS between different kinds of inference, deduction and interpretation, skills which are an important part of learning for this age group.

**Figure 4.13   PIRLS processes and National Curriculum assessment focuses**

| PIRLS processes of comprehension | National Curriculum assessment focuses |
|---|---|
| Focus on and retrieve explicitly stated information and ideas | *Assessment focus 2*: understand, describe, select or retrieve information, events or ideas from texts and use quotation and reference to text |
| Make straightforward inferences | *Assessment focus 3*: Deduce, infer or interpret information, events or ideas from texts |
| Interpret and integrate ideas and information | *Assessment focus 3*: Deduce, infer or interpret information, events or ideas from texts |
| Examine and evaluate content, language and textual elements | *Assessment focus 4*: identify and comment on the structure and organisation of texts, including grammatical and presentational features at text level<br><br>*Assessment focus 5*: explain and comment on writers' use of language, including grammatical and literary features at word and sentence level<br><br>*Assessment focus 6*: identify and comment on writers' purposes and viewpoints and the effect of the text on the reader<br><br>*Assessment focus 7*: relate texts to their social, cultural and historical contexts and literary traditions |

To examine how these similarities and contrasts work out in practice, the PIRLS assessment can be compared with the National Curriculum reading test taken by these same children a year later. This test, entitled *Fire – Friend or Foe?* is based on a reading booklet containing four different texts: a double-page spread of information about the beneficial effects of forest fires; a poem; an extract from a novel; and a newspaper article. A range of literary and non-literary text types was therefore included, as in PIRLS. In National Curriculum tests, there are no predetermined proportions of literary and informational texts, unlike PIRLS. A further difference is that, in *Fire – Friend or Foe?* children are asked questions requiring them to look across the different texts, whereas in PIRLS each set of questions refers to only one text. Commentaries on these questions are drawn from the national analysis of standards (QCA, 2003).

*Fire – Friend or Foe?* includes some simple multiple choice or written questions that correspond to the first of the PIRLS processes, *Focus on and retrieve explicitly stated information and ideas,* for example:

The flames move quickly because of

the animals      the sun      the wind      the smoke

> Find and copy a phrase on page 10 which tells you that the impala doe and her baby were safe.

About 20 per cent of the marks in the test are for questions of this type. The first of these questions is an example that most level 3 children in the national tests – those below the expected level in England – were able to answer well.

There are also questions corresponding to the *Make straightforward inferences* process. In one example, children have to show that they have grasped the basic ideas of the poem by working out that the animals are escaping from a forest fire, and that they are searching for safety near water:

> In the poem, what are the forest animals
>
> a) escaping from?
>
> b) looking for?

These questions account for about 28 per cent of the marks in *Fire – Friend or Foe?* The national analysis of the test reports that almost all children who achieved level 4 were able to answer this question correctly. Level 3 children did well on the first part, but found the second part more difficult.

The national test also includes questions requiring complex inferences to be made, based on an overview of the whole text, and corresponding quite closely to the PIRLS category *Interpret and integrate ideas and information.* Examples of these are:

> What is the main idea of the second verse of the poem?
>
> the speed and heat of the fire ☐
>
> the size and depth of the river ☐
>
> the fear and urgency of the animals ☐
>
> the thirst and hunger of the animals ☐

> *He was still too young to be afraid* (page 9)
>
> Explain what this means and why it is important to the story.

The QCA analysis shows that around two-thirds of children achieving level 4 were successful in the first of these questions. For the second, level 4 children tended to gain partial credit by giving imprecise answers, and even those at level 5 found it rather difficult to give a full explanation.

In this category, too, are the questions requiring children to bring together information, not just from within one text, but across the variety of texts included in the reading booklet. This is the final question in the test:

> The reading booklet is called *Fire – Friend or Foe?*
>
> Think about everything you have read in the reading booklet and explain why this is a good title.

This question carries three marks, and for full credit pupils have to explain the ideas in the title, making reference to both the positive and negative effects of forest fires and referring to at least two of the texts they have read. Because of this need to integrate ideas across texts, rather than just within a single text, questions of this kind can be seen as more demanding than any of those in PIRLS. It is typical of performance at level 5: in the national analysis, almost half of level 5 children gained full marks, as against only a very small proportion of level 4 pupils. In total, complex inference questions account for about 30 per cent of marks in *Fire – Friend or Foe?*

The fourth process in PIRLS is *Examine and evaluate content, language and textual elements.* This includes a variety of different types of questions and, although questions in the National Curriculum test can be assigned to this category, the balance and nature of the demands upon pupils are not as easily mapped as for the other three PIRLS processes (see Figure 4.13). In PIRLS, for example, this category of question includes:

> Would you like to go and rescue pufflings with Halla and her friends?
>
> Use what you have read to help you explain.

while other questions require analysis of the organisation of information – for example, identifying the persuasive and information-giving parts of the *River Trail* leaflet. Because of the difficulties of translation in an international test, very few PIRLS questions address the author's choice of language or use of imagery.

In *Fire – Friend or Foe?* questions that can be assigned to this category sometimes require an analysis of the organisation of the writing or the techniques used by the author:

> What do the arrows show you about the structure of the text?

> Why do you think the writer used the word *terror*?

In this category, too, there are questions in the national test that are more demanding than any in PIRLS:

> Look at the three paragraphs on page 8 starting from
>
> > *Out of the grass …*
>
> How does the writer build up the sense of fear as the fire approaches?

To gain the full three marks, it is necessary to identify three separate authorial techniques that contribute towards this effect, such as describing aspects of the fire, using specific vocabulary, highlighting the animals' demonstration of fear. This question proved difficult even for children achieving level 5 overall. Questions that can be classified under this PIRLS process account for about 22 per cent of the marks in the national test.

In summary, then, the skills and understandings that are taught through the National Curriculum and assessed in the national test have a fairly close relationship to those included in the PIRLS assessment, and when the questions are roughly classified using the PIRLS categories the proportions are very similar. However, there are also some notable differences. In PIRLS, children are offered a multiple choice format to help them structure their responses for about 50 per cent of the available marks, whereas in the national test the proportion is much lower, at about 18 per cent. There is no more than one three-mark extended question in each PIRLS block, whereas *Fire – Friend or Foe?* includes three of these. Some of the questions in the national tests make demonstrably greater demands on children than anything in PIRLS, requiring integration of ideas across texts and in-depth analysis of authorial techniques. It must, of course, be borne in mind that the national tests are taken in year 6, when children are a full year older than when they participated in the PIRLS study.

Overall, the high performance of children in England on the PIRLS assessment can be seen as related to the broad reading literacy curriculum that they follow in key stage 2. Both in the range of texts and in the inferential and analytic comprehension skills taught, the curriculum reinforces and goes beyond the demands of the PIRLS reading literacy tests.

# 5.  The Pupils and the Home

As part of the PIRLS survey, questionnaires were completed by pupils and their parents.  They were asked a series of questions about their reading habits, the reading resources available in their homes and their background. This chapter presents their responses and cross-references them with information about the average reading achievement of the pupils. International comparisons are made where relevant.

- The parents who responded to the questionnaire in England tended to be those with higher achieving children.  Their homes have, on average, a very high level of educational resources.

- Parents have a very positive attitude to reading and expose their children to a high level of literacy activity before they start school (for example, reading stories, playing word games), which declines as the children get older.

- Despite a higher score on the international reading assessment, ten-year-old pupils in England have a poorer attitude towards reading, and read less often for fun than similar pupils in other countries.  Boys have a less positive attitude to reading than girls.

- Ten-year-old children in England tend to play computer games more frequently than their international peers, watch television more frequently and for longer.

## 5.1    The pupils

### Pupil attitudes to reading

The revised National Curriculum for English (2000) emphasises the need to encourage positive attitudes towards reading as a major objective.  Key stage 1 aims to develop children's interest and pleasure in reading as they learn to read confidently and independently, and an objective at key stage 2 is that pupils should read enthusiastically a range of materials and use their knowledge of words, sentences and texts to understand and respond to meaning.  Children who enjoy reading read more frequently and thus expand their range of reading experiences and improve their skills of comprehension.

To investigate year 5 attitudes to reading, PIRLS created an index based on children's responses to the following statements: *I read only if I have to, I like talking about books with*

*other people, I would be happy if someone gave me a book as a present, I think reading is boring,* and *I enjoy reading.* Responses to each statement were assigned a score ranging from 4 points for 'agree a lot' to 1 point for 'disagree a lot', and were averaged. Responses for negative statements were reverse coded. Pupils were then placed in one of three categories, high, medium or low, according to their responses. Those in the high category tended to agree or agree a lot with all of the statements. Those in the low category tended to disagree or disagree a lot with all of the statements. Those in the medium category were pupils who gave mixed responses to the questions. Table 5.1 shows the percentage of pupils in each of the three categories together with their average performance on the PIRLS reading assessment.

**Table 5.1   Index of pupils' attitudes towards reading**

| High | | Medium | | Low | |
|---|---|---|---|---|---|
| Per cent of pupils | Average achievement | Per cent of pupils | Average achievement | Per cent of pupils | Average achievement |
| 44 | 584 | 43 | 531 | 13 | 521 |
| (51) | (524) | (43) | (479) | (6) | (478) |

N = 3156; (international average)

Of note is the relatively poor rating of the pupils from England on the attitude index compared with international average outcomes. For England, 44 per cent of the pupils were placed in the high category and 87 per cent were in either the medium or high categories. Internationally, about half (51 per cent) of all students were placed in the high category and over 90 per cent were in either the medium or high categories. Within all countries in PIRLS, children who have more positive attitudes to reading tend to also have higher scores. However, countries which have the highest proportion of pupils with the most positive attitudes do not have the highest scale scores on PIRLS.

The percentage of pupils from Sweden in the high category was three points above the international average, but The Netherlands, the other country ranked above England in the overall Reading Achievement scale, recorded 43 per cent of pupils in that category. Scotland (47 per cent) and the United States (42 per cent) were among other countries scoring below the international average on this index.

Also of note are the 13 per cent of pupils in England in the low category of the attitude index against an international average of 6 per cent. This percentage was the same as for the United States and exceeded only by The Netherlands (15 per cent). Broken down by gender, 8 per cent of girls in England came within the low category, a proportion equal in size only to United States, and 18 per cent of boys came within the same category, which was exceeded only by the United States (19 per cent) and The Netherlands (23 per cent).

As in all countries in the survey, girls in England had more positive attitudes to reading, as measured by the index, than boys: 53 per cent of girls and 35 per cent of boys were in the high category against an international average of 60 per cent and 42 per cent. The difference between the percentage of boys and girls in England with the most positive reading attitudes at 18 per cent, was the same as the international average. There is, however, no statistically significant relationship between a country's overall reading achievement on PIRLS and the attitude to reading of the pupils.

When asked the extent to which they thought they needed to read well for their future, 64 per cent of the pupils agreed a lot that they did and 22 per cent agreed a little. Internationally, 75 per cent and 16 per cent of pupils respectively chose these options.

## Pupils' reading confidence

In addition to the index of pupils' attitudes towards reading, PIRLS constructed an index of reading self-concept or confidence. This was intended to examine pupils' conceptions of their reading ability in the belief that positive perceptions may influence pupils' perseverance with a task or may encourage their engagement in activities related to academic performance. Pupils were asked to respond to the following statements about how well they read: *reading is very easy for me, I do not read as well as other students in my class*, and *reading aloud is very hard for me*. As with the previous index, pupils were asked to indicate their responses on a 4-point scale ranging from 'agree a lot' to 'disagree a lot'. Pupils placed in the high category tended to agree or agree a lot with all the statements. Pupils in the low category tended to disagree or disagree a lot with all the statements. Pupils in the medium category were those who gave mixed combinations of responses to these questions. The information from the index is summarised in Table 5.2 which also provides average scores from the PIRLS reading assessment.

**Table 5.2   Index of pupils' reading confidence**

| High | | Medium | | Low | |
|---|---|---|---|---|---|
| Per cent of pupils | Average achievement | Per cent of pupils | Average achievement | Per cent of pupils | Average achievement |
| 33 | 588 | 58 | 542 | 9 | 493 |
| (40) | (530) | (55) | (485) | (5) | (457) |

N = 3156; (international average)

For England, 33 per cent of pupils were in the high category of the pupils' index of reading confidence and 91 per cent came within the medium and high categories combined. These figures compare with an international average of 40 per cent and 95 per cent respectively. Both for England (58 per cent), and internationally (55 per cent), the majority of pupils were in the medium category. Within all countries in the PIRLS survey, pupils with a higher level of reading confidence had higher achievement in the reading assessment. Of note is the relatively low reading confidence of the children in England which, measured in terms of the average international performance, is disproportionate to their comparatively high point scores on the reading assessment.

Unlike the majority of countries in the survey, the results for England on the index of reading confidence did not show any significant differences between boys and girls in the high or medium categories.

## Pupils' reading habits

To find out about pupils' reading habits, the PIRLS pupil questionnaire asked a series of questions about how frequently children read outside school and what texts they read. Table 5.3 shows how frequently pupils read outside school.

**Table 5.3   Frequency of reading outside school for fun**

| Every day or almost every day | | Once or twice a week | | Once or twice a month | | Never or almost never | |
|---|---|---|---|---|---|---|---|
| Per cent of pupils | Average achievement | Per cent of pupils | Average achievement | Per cent of pupils | Average achievement | Per cent of pupils | Average achievement |
| 33 | 583 | 26 | 554 | 14 | 555 | 27 | 516 |
| (40) | (515) | (29) | (501) | (12) | (492) | (18) | (478) |

N = 3156; (international average)

Unsurprisingly, in England, children who read most frequently for fun were also those with the highest scores on PIRLS, mirroring the situation on average internationally. As was observed with reading attitudes and confidence, whilst within the majority of countries there was an association between frequency of reading for fun and achievement, between countries there was no clear association. The countries with the highest percentages of children who claimed to read for fun every day or almost every day were the Russian Federation (59 per cent), Lithuania (53 per cent), Iceland (52 per cent) and Bulgaria (51 per cent).

Thirty-one per cent of children in Scotland reported reading for fun every day or almost every day, as did 37 per cent in The Netherlands and 44 per cent in Sweden. Scotland and Italy had the highest proportion of children who reported never or almost never reading for fun (35 per cent) with 34 per cent in The Netherlands and 11 per cent in Sweden.

An index was constructed which summarised pupils' responses to questions about what they read for information outside school. They were asked how often they read to find out about things they wanted to learn, how often they read books that explain things, magazines, newspapers, and directions or instructions. Responses were averaged and are shown in Table 5.4. This table also shows the frequency of pupils reading novels or stories.

**Table 5.4   Frequency of reading for different purposes outside school**

| | Every day or almost every day | | Once or twice a week | | Once or twice a month | | Never or almost never | |
|---|---|---|---|---|---|---|---|---|
| Frequency of reading for: | Per cent of pupils | Average achievement | Per cent of pupils | Average achievement | Per cent of pupils | Average-achievement | Per cent of pupils | Average achievement |
| information | 12 | 530 | 43 | 548 | 37 | 568 | 8 | 549 |
| | (18) | (494) | (43) | (504) | (31) | (504) | (9) | (490) |
| stories or novels | 38 | 574 | 32 | 553 | 17 | 547 | 13 | 501 |
| | (32) | (512) | (31) | (501) | (18) | (500) | (19) | (478) |

N = 3156; (international average)

Pupils in England are more likely to read stories and novels outside school than they are to read information books. This is broadly in line with the international picture. The relationship between reading outside school and achievement is a complex one. Children who read novels most frequently outside school tended to score more highly than those who read them less frequently, but the evidence suggests a different pattern for the index of frequency of reading information texts. Reading these very frequently is associated with lower scores than reading them weekly or monthly, in England and internationally.

Broken down by gender, 45 per cent of girls (38 per cent on average internationally) read a story or novel outside school every day or almost every day compared with 29 per cent of boys (26 per cent internationally). There was no significant difference between boys and girls in the frequency of reading for information. This gender difference goes some way to explaining the difference in the scale scores of pupils who report reading novels and stories frequently and those who report reading them very rarely.

In other higher attaining countries, children in Sweden and Bulgaria reported reading stories and novels less frequently than children in England whilst those in The Netherlands read them more frequently.

Pupils in The Netherlands and Sweden reported doing relatively little reading for information and less frequently than reported by pupils in England. These countries had the smallest percentage of pupils, four and six per cent respectively, who reported reading for information on average every day or almost every day. Children in Bulgaria reported reading information texts more frequently than children in England, and had very similar ratings to the international average.

Some 46 per cent of pupils in England (with a mean PIRLS scale score of 543) reported borrowing books to read for fun from school or public libraries at least once a week and 36 per cent (573) reported borrowing books once or twice a month. This was marginally above the international average of 43 per cent (498) and 32 per cent (506) respectively. Pupils reporting that they never or almost never borrowed books in this way represented 19 per cent (539) from England and 24 per cent (496) internationally. There is no clear link between reading achievement and library usage.

### Time spent playing computer games or watching television or videos

In addition to asking about their reading habits, the PIRLS questionnaire asked children about the time they spent playing computer games or watching television or videos. Table 5.5 shows the frequency with which pupils played computer games and their average achievement on the reading assessment.

**Table 5.5   Frequency of playing computer games**

| Every day or almost every day | | Once or twice a week | | Once or twice a month | | Never or almost never | |
|---|---|---|---|---|---|---|---|
| Per cent of pupils | Average achievement | Per cent of pupils | Average achievement | Per cent of pupils | Average achievement | Per cent of pupils | Average achievement |
| 40 | 536 | 38 | 564 | 12 | 582 | 7 | 549 |
| (26) | (498) | (26) | (515) | (11) | (520) | (8) | (489) |

N = 3156; (international average)

England's high percentage of pupils playing computer games every day (40 per cent) was significantly above the international average (26 per cent) and only exceeded by three countries in the international sample: Israel (61 per cent), The Netherlands (42 per cent) and

Scotland (41 per cent). It can be seen that pupils in England who played computer games most frequently achieved a lower average score on the reading assessment than the other groups.

Table 5.6 records how often children reported watching television or videos on a normal school day and their average score on the reading assessment, whereas Table 5.7 details the length of time children spend watching television or videos on a normal school day, together with their average scores from the PIRLS assessment.

**Table 5.6   Frequency of watching television or videos**

| Every day or almost every day | | Once or twice a week | | Once or twice a month | | Never or almost never | |
|---|---|---|---|---|---|---|---|
| Per cent of pupils | Average achievement | Per cent of pupils | Average achievement | Per cent of pupils | Average achievement | Per cent of pupils | Average achievement |
| 80 | 560 | 12 | 549 | 3 | 546 | 5 | 454 |
| (63) | (507) | (21) | (502) | (7) | (493) | (9) | (469) |

N = 3156; (international average)

Eighty per cent of pupils in England reported that they watched television or videos every day or almost every day, a figure exceeded within the sampled countries by the Slovak Republic alone (82 per cent). The international average was 63 per cent. The most frequent television watchers in England also had the highest scores on the reading assessment.

**Table 5.7   Length of time spent watching television or videos**

| 5 hours or more | | From 3 hours to 5 hours | | From 1 hour to 3 hours | | Less than 1 hour | | Average hours per day |
|---|---|---|---|---|---|---|---|---|
| Per cent of pupils | Average achievement | Per cent of pupils | Average achievement | Per cent of pupils | Average achievement | Per cent of pupils | Average achievement | |
| 20 | 522 | 17 | 569 | 36 | 569 | 27 | 544 | 2.6 |
| (12) | (482) | (12) | (500) | (33) | (511) | (43) | (407) | (2.0) |

N = 3156; (international average)

Whereas watching television every day or nearly every day is associated with those children who also scored the highest average points on the reading assessment, this does not hold for the length of time spent watching television or videos. Those children who claim to watch television for more than five hours on a normal school day achieved lower scores on average than pupils who watched for shorter periods. This pattern of findings is largely replicated in the average international figures.

## 5.2    The home

To provide information about pupils' early literacy activities that would help to interpret their reading achievement results, PIRLS collected information from parents about their background, their own reading, their children's early home experiences in learning to read, and about the literacy resources available in the home.  Although a response rate of 55 per cent to the home questionnaire would normally be seen as good, it is lower than that achieved by most other countries in PIRLS.  What is of more importance than the absolute number of questionnaires returned, however, is the apparent unrepresentativeness of the respondents. The mean scale score of pupils whose parents returned the questionnaire was 574, against 530 for pupils whose parents did not respond.  This must be considered when data from the home questionnaire is being interpreted.  Two countries, Morocco and the United States, did not administer the home questionnaire.

### Parental attitudes to reading

Parents were asked how much time they spent reading for themselves at home including books, magazines, newspapers and materials for work.  Table 5.8 summarises the percentage of pupils whose parents responded in each category, together with the average reading achievement of the pupils.

**Table 5.8    Parents' reading at home**

| More than 10 hours a week | | 6–10 hours a week | | 1–5 hours a week | | Less than one hour a week | |
|---|---|---|---|---|---|---|---|
| Per cent of pupils | Average achievement | Per cent of pupils | Average achievement | Per cent of pupils | Average achievement | Per cent of pupils | Average achievement |
| 22 | 591 | 30 | 581 | 39 | 563 | 9 | 529 |
| (17) | (524) | (24) | (520) | (41) | (505) | (19) | (478) |

Data available for 50–69 per cent of pupils; (international average)

On average 52 per cent of pupils in England had a parent who reported reading for six or more hours a week compared to an international average of 41 per cent.  Reading achievement was highest among those pupils whose parents read the most.

Parents were also asked how often they read for enjoyment at home.  For England, 56 per cent of pupils had a parent who reported reading every day or almost every day for pleasure, against an international average of 45 per cent.  As with the previous measure, reading achievement was highest amongst those pupils whose parents read for pleasure most frequently, with the highest achievement (scale score of 582) being associated with those who read for pleasure every day (international average scale score of 516) and the lowest achievement (scale score of 533) with those who never or almost never read for pleasure (international average scale score of 484).

To investigate parents' attitudes towards reading, PIRLS constructed an index based on their responses to the following five statements: *I read only if I have to, I like talking about books with other people, I like to spend my spare time reading, I read only if I need information,* and *reading is an important activity in my home.*  Their responses, on a four point scale ranging from 'agree a lot' to 'disagree a lot', were given a numeric code and averaged across the five statements.  Pupils were then assigned to one of three categories, high, medium or low, on the basis of their parents' average response. Pupils in the high category had parents who tended to agree a little or a lot with the five statements. Pupils in the low category had parents who, on average, disagreed a lot with the statements. Pupils in the medium category had parents whose responses fell between those extremes.

Table 5.9 presents the percentage of pupils at each level of the index together with the average reading achievement of those pupils.

**Table 5.9  Index of parents' attitudes toward reading**

| High parental attitude to reading | | Medium parental attitude to reading | | Low parental attitude to reading | |
|---|---|---|---|---|---|
| Per cent of pupils | Average achievement | Per cent of pupils | Average achievement | Per cent of pupils | Average achievement |
| 69 | 586 | 26 | 543 | 6 | 535 |
| (53) | (524) | (42) | (492) | (5) | (482) |

Data available for 50–69 per cent of pupils; (international average)

The parents from the England sample demonstrated very favourable attitudes toward reading with 69 per cent of the pupils in the high category of the index, 26 per cent in the middle category and 6 per cent in the low category. Comparable international figures were 53, 42 and 5 per cent. Pupils from England in the high level of the index had higher average reading achievement (scale score of 586) than pupils at the medium (scale score of 543) or low (scale score of 535) level.

## Early literacy experiences at home

To investigate the early literacy experiences of pupils in the sample, PIRLS created an index of home literacy activities by asking parents how often they, or someone else in the home, engaged in a range of activities with their child before they began school. The six activities for which information was collected were: read books, tell stories, sing songs, play with alphabet toys, play word games, and read aloud signs and labels.

Responses about each activity from the parents' questionnaire were recorded on a three-point scale: often, sometimes and never or almost never. The index was constructed by averaging responses across the six activities and assigning pupils to one of three categories, high, medium or low, on the basis of their parents' average response. Pupils in the high category had parents who reported that they tended to often engage in the six activities. Pupils in the low category had parents who reported that they tended never or almost never to engage in the activities. Pupils in the medium category had parents reporting in between these extremes. Table 5.10 presents the percentage of pupils in each category of the early home literacy activities index together with the average reading achievement of those pupils.

Parents in England reported the highest level of engagement with their child in pre-school literacy activities of all the countries in the survey and were closely followed by Scotland (82 per cent). Another English-speaking country, New Zealand (68 per cent), was third in terms of the percentage of pupils in the high category of the index. It should be noted that the four countries with the highest scores on this index had response rates to the parent questionnaire of between 50 and 84 per cent of pupils, and the data derived from the questionnaire may be unrepresentative. There was a positive relationship within all countries in the survey between engaging in early learning activities and performance on the

PIRLS reading assessment, although the countries with the highest average reading achievement were not necessarily those with the highest percentages of pupils in the high category of the index. Sweden, the highest performing country, had 41 per cent and The Netherlands, the next highest, had 55 per cent. Pupils in the high category for England gained a 32-point advantage in reading performance over peers in the medium category who, in turn, had scale scores 33 points above pupils in the low category. This advantage was higher than the average across all countries in the survey which was 21 and 18 points respectively.

**Table 5.10   Index of early home literacy activities**

| High level of early home literacy activities | | Medium level of early home literacy activities | | Low level of early home literacy activities | |
|---|---|---|---|---|---|
| Per cent of pupils | Average achievement | Per cent of pupils | Average achievement | Per cent of pupils | Average achievement |
| 83 | 578 | 14 | 546 | 3 | 513 |
| (52) | (520) | (35) | (499) | (13) | (481) |

Data available for 50–69 per cent of pupils; (international average)

Taking one element of the index, reading books to the child before school entry, the pattern of results for England is similar to the outcome of the overall index with 82 per cent of parents reporting that they often read to their child (51 per cent international average), with an associated PIRLS scale score of 581 (international average 522). The percentage in this category for England is the largest of all the countries in the survey, equalled only by Iceland but closely followed by Scotland (79 per cent) and New Zealand (76 per cent). The Netherlands, Sweden and Norway, each with 70 per cent, recorded the next highest percentages in this category. Only one per cent of parents in England reported that they never or almost never read a book to their pre-school child, the countries recording the highest percentages being Iran (28 per cent) and Turkey (25 per cent) against an international average of seven per cent. Across all the countries in the survey, the association between often reading a book with the child and high reading performance is more clear-cut than with the index as a whole.

Parents were also asked how often they, or someone else in the household, watched television programmes with the child that taught reading. The results are shown in Table 5.11.

**Table 5.11   Parents watching television programmes with the pre-school child that teach reading**

| Often | | Sometimes | | Never or almost never | |
|---|---|---|---|---|---|
| Per cent of pupils | Average achievement | Per cent of pupils | Average achievement | Per cent of pupils | Average achievement |
| 67 | 570 | 28 | 578 | 5 | 556 |
| (36) | (507) | (35) | (507) | (29) | (505) |

Data available for 50–69 per cent of pupils; (international average)

A number of countries, including The Netherlands, Norway, Sweden and Scotland, had ratings of over 90 per cent for the proportion of pupils whose parents reported that they often or sometimes watched television programmes with their child that taught reading. Only Norway (97 per cent) recorded a higher percentage of parents watching such programmes with their children sometimes or often than England (95 per cent). The international average was 71 per cent. However, there was no association between the three categories in terms of reading achievement.

Far fewer parents, in England and internationally, reported engaging in early reading activities on the computer with their pre-school child (Table 5.12) compared to the proportions reporting watching television programmes concerned with the teaching of reading.

**Table 5.12   Parents using early reading activities on computer with the pre-school child**

| Often | | Sometimes | | Never or almost never | |
|---|---|---|---|---|---|
| Per cent of pupils | Average achievement | Per cent of pupils | Average achievement | Per cent of pupils | Average achievement |
| 8 | 580 | 25 | 571 | 66 | 572 |
| (5) | (505) | (15) | (512) | (79) | (506) |

Data available for 50–69 per cent of pupils; (international average)

Parents of the PIRLS year 5 pupils were asked how well their child could do each of the following five activities when they began year 1 (compared to 1st grade internationally): recognise most of the letters in the alphabet, write letters of the alphabet, read some words, write some words and read sentences. Their responses were averaged across the five activities and the results are shown in Table 5.13.

**Table 5.13   How well pupils could do early literacy activities on starting school (based on parents' reports)**

| Very well | | Moderately well | | Not very well | | Not at all | |
|---|---|---|---|---|---|---|---|
| Per cent of pupils | Average achievement | Per cent of pupils | Average achievement | Per cent of pupils | Average achievement | Per cent of pupils | Average achievement |
| 29 | 602 | 43 | 572 | 22 | 543 | 6 | 523 |
| (21) | (537) | (33) | (511) | (29) | (491) | (17) | (478) |

Data available for 50–69 per cent of pupils; (international average)

The parents' responses are not directly comparable with those of the headteachers reported in Chapter 6 below since the parents were responding about individual children, whereas the headteachers were responding about the pupils in the school as a whole. In England, 72 per cent of the parents felt their children could perform the activities moderately or very well, against an international average of 54 per cent. Parents' reports of their children's early literacy skills fit well with the pupils' subsequent performance on the PIRLS reading assessment.

## Later literacy experiences at home

Parents were also asked about more recent reading activities which they did with their child. Table 5.14 records the current level of activity in a range of areas such as reading aloud to the child, listening to reading, talking about reading and going to the library. The associated average reading achievement of the children in each category is also shown.

**Table 5.14  Parental/guardian activity with child in reading-related activities**

| Parent: | Every day or almost every day | | Once or twice a week | | Once or twice a month | | Never or almost never | |
|---|---|---|---|---|---|---|---|---|
| | Per cent of pupils | Average achievement | Per cent of pupils | Average achievement | Per cent of pupils | Average achievement | Per cent of pupils | Average achievement |
| reads aloud to child | 22 | 567 | 39 | 560 | 25 | 579 | 15 | 596 |
| | (23) | (504) | (37) | (502) | (21) | (512) | (19) | (517) |
| listens to child reading | 29 | 557 | 47 | 567 | 20 | 594 | 5 | 606 |
| | (40) | (501) | (38) | (509) | (15) | (519) | (7) | (516) |
| talks about child's reading | 30 | 572 | 54 | 571 | 14 | 574 | 3 | 5 |
| | (34) | (507) | (42) | (510) | (17) | (509) | (7) | (490) |
| talks to child about own reading | 13 | 559 | 40 | 575 | 29 | 575 | 18 | 567 |
| | (18) | (502) | (34) | (508) | (26) | (514) | (22) | (504) |
| discusses class reading with child | 32 | 562 | 43 | 573 | 20 | 580 | 5 | 585 |
| | (43) | (503) | (32) | (508) | (16) | (511) | (9) | (507) |
| goes to library with child | 2 | 544 | 17 | 571 | 65 | 579 | 16 | 546 |
| | (4) | (499) | (15) | (514) | (44) | (518) | (36) | (493) |

Data available for 50–69 per cent of pupils; (international average)

Combining responses relating to activities that take place once or twice a week or daily, it can be seen that the percentage of parents undertaking a range of reading-related activities with their children is similar to the international averages in each of the activities listed. The higher than international average level of pre-school literacy activity reported by parents in England is not continued into formal primary schooling. Of note is that the positive relationship between early learning activities and performance on the PIRLS reading assessment is not evidenced with regard to the six reading-related activities listed here. As with the pupil-reported library use, there is no association between going to the library with a parent and reading achievement scores. There is some suggestion that in most countries, including England, the weakest readers tend to read aloud at home most frequently.

## Educational resources in the home

PIRLS developed an index of home educational resources based on parents' and pupils' reports of the number of books, the number of children's books, and the presence of four educational aids (computer, study desk for own use, books of their own, and access to a daily newspaper) in the home and on parents' education. Pupils assigned to the high level of this index reported coming from homes with more than 100 books, more than 25 children's books, at least three of the four educational aids, and where at least one parent had finished university. Pupils assigned to the low level had 25 or fewer books in the home, 25 or fewer children's books, no more than two of the four educational aids, and parents who had not completed secondary education. The remaining pupils were assigned to the medium level. Table 5.15 shows the percentage of pupils at each level of the index together with the average reading achievement for those pupils. international averages are also shown. As previously, the potential unrepresentativeness of the data from the home questionnaire in England needs to be considered when this table is interpreted.

**Table 5.15   Index of home educational resources**

| High | | Medium | | Low | |
|---|---|---|---|---|---|
| Per cent of pupils | Average achievement | Per cent of pupils | Average achievement | Per cent of pupils | Average achievement |
| 27 | 584 | 69 | 547 | 4 | 479 |
| (13) | (548) | (74) | (504) | (13) | (443) |

Data available for 50–69 per cent of pupils; (international average)

England had the third highest proportion of pupils in the high category behind the United States (37 per cent) and Norway (33 per cent). The difference between the average reading achievement in the high category and the low category is substantial (105 points). This difference for England is the same as the international average. Having children's books in the home may be more important for fostering literacy among young children than having books in general. About a third of parents responding to the questionnaire in a number of countries (Canada, England, Iceland, New Zealand, Norway and Sweden) reported on average more than 100 children's books in the home.

# 6.  The Teachers and the Schools

**Questionnaires were sent to teachers and to headteachers to collect information about the pupils and the schools they attended, the teachers who taught them and about how reading was taught.  The international comparisons arising from these responses were supplemented in England by specific questions about the national literacy strategy.**

■ Children in England start school earlier, show more reading readiness and have a higher level of early learning skills than their international peers.  They are taught for more hours, in larger classes and by teachers who are more highly qualified.  England is amongst the countries with the highest numbers of books in schools and the best access to specialist staff for the teaching of reading.

■ More pupils in England are taught using a variety of grouping arrangements than elsewhere and children of different reading abilities are more likely to use different materials.  Children in England were more likely than those in any other country in PIRLS to be taught by teachers who use a variety of children's books in their teaching of reading.

■ Teachers found the resource materials and training provided for the national literacy strategy (NLS) useful.  Guided reading sessions were frequently used by teachers in the survey, who recorded broad agreement about the activities within these sessions.  Teachers believe that the NLS has introduced pupils to a wider range of texts.

■ Ten-year-old pupils in England are likely to have less reading homework and their parents to have less formal involvement with the schools than the international average.

■ The range of reading ability in rural and urban schools, and in schools with the highest and lowest proportions of economically disadvantaged pupils, is wider than in most other countries.

■ Children in England are amongst those with the greatest access to computers and to the Internet of any in the survey.

# 6.1    The teachers

The PIRLS survey collected background characteristics of the teachers of the year 5 (4th grade) pupils. Although the policy varied greatly across the countries in the survey, year 5 pupils in England generally stay with the same teacher for one school year (88 per cent compared to an international average of 31 per cent). This is similar to the pattern in the United States (95 per cent) and Canada (91 per cent). Internationally, many students (27 per cent) stay with the same teacher for four or more years. About half of the pupils in England spend all or most of their time during that year with one teacher (52 per cent) and about one-third (30 per cent) have different teachers for different subjects. These figures are very similar to the international averages (54 per cent and 32 per cent respectively).

In England, 80 per cent of the teachers of this age group were female, the majority were between 40 and 49 years of age, had been teaching for 14 years and had 5 years' experience of teaching this age group. This profile is typical of the international average as illustrated by Table 6.1. The percentage of year 5 (4th grade) pupils taught by teachers under the age of 30 is, however, greater in England than internationally.

**Table 6.1    Teachers' gender, age and teaching experience**

| Percentage of pupils by teacher characteristics | | | | | | Number of years teaching | |
|---|---|---|---|---|---|---|---|
| Gender | | Age | | | | | |
| Female | Male | 29 years or under | 30–39 years | 40–49 years | 50 years or older | All years | Year 5 (4th grade) |
| 80 | 20 | 28 | 16 | 36 | 20 | 14 | 5 |
| (81) | (19) | (19) | (29) | (30) | (22) | (16) | (5) |

Data: Teachers' questionnaire; (international average)

In only three countries, England, New Zealand and the United States, were all the pupils in the sample taught by teachers with a university degree. Internationally, 65 per cent of pupils were taught by graduates.

# 6.2    The schools

## School characteristics

Table 6.2 shows the location of the schools attended by the pupils in the survey, categorised by whether they are urban, suburban or rural schools. Average attainment on the PIRLS reading assessment is provided for each group of pupils.

**Table 6.2    School locations**

| Urban | | Suburban | | Rural | |
|---|---|---|---|---|---|
| Per cent of pupils | Average achievement | Per cent of pupils | Average achievement | Per cent of pupils | Average achievement |
| 48 | 542 | 32 | 557 | 21 | 574 |
| (46) | (507) | (25) | (502) | (29) | (485) |

Data: Headteachers' questionnaire; (international average)

In England, children in rural schools had higher average scores than children in suburban schools, who in turn had higher average scores than children in urban schools. England was one of only two countries where this pattern was observed: internationally, children in rural schools had the lowest mean score and those in urban schools the highest.

Headteachers were asked to report on the proportion of pupils in their schools from economically disadvantaged homes. Table 6.3 shows the percentage of year 5 pupils in the survey in each of the categories used, together with their average reading achievement on the PIRLS assessment.

**Table 6.3   Pupils from economically disadvantaged homes**

| 0–10 economically disadvantaged | | 11–25 per cent economically disadvantaged | | 26–50 per cent economically disadvantaged | | More than 50 per cent economically disadvantaged | |
|---|---|---|---|---|---|---|---|
| Per cent of pupils | Average achievement | Per cent of pupils | Average achievement | Per cent of pupils | Average achievement | Per cent of pupils | Average achievement |
| 34 | 578 | 34 | 557 | 18 | 532 | 13 | 511 |
| (33) | (518) | (24) | (505) | (20) | (493) | (23) | (478) |

Data: Headteachers' questionnaire; (international average)

Approximately one-third of pupils in England attended schools where more than a quarter of the pupils came from what the headteachers considered to be economically disadvantaged backgrounds, 12 per cent fewer than the international average. The average achievement of pupils on the reading assessment decreases as the percentage of economically disadvantaged pupils in the school increases. Of note is the difference between the most and least disadvantaged categories in the average pupil reading achievement scores for England and internationally: 67 score points and 40 points respectively.

The range of average reading ability in urban and rural schools and in schools with higher or lower levels of economic disadvantage is considerably wider in England than the international average.

## Pre-school

Pupils in the PIRLS countries mostly began primary education when they were six or seven years old. In England, nearly all pupils began primary education when they were five. There is no clear relationship from the PIRLS data between the age of entry to primary schooling and year 5 reading achievement. Among the top-performing countries on the PIRLS reading assessment, for example, the pupils in Sweden started primary school when they were seven, and those in The Netherlands and England when they were five (Mullis *et al*, 2002). It should be noted, however, that in Sweden there is extensive kindergarten provision where children are taught skills on a systematic basis. In England, nursery provision is available free of charge to all four-year-olds whose parents want it. According to data from the PIRLS home questionnaire, 12 per cent of the pupils in England did not attend pre-primary education, 26 per cent attended for up to and including one year, 45 per cent attended for more than one year up to and including two years and 18 per cent attended for more than two years. Attendance at pre-school over a longer period was associated with higher scores in PIRLS, in England and in many other countries. The PIRLS survey did not collect information about how many sessions a week a child attended pre-primary provision.

nfer

## Reading readiness

Headteachers were asked in the PIRLS questionnaire to estimate how many of their pupils were ready to begin learning in a formal setting when they began school (year 1 in England). They were asked what proportion of their pupils beginning the first year of school could: recognise most of the alphabet, read some words, read sentences, write letters of the alphabet and write some words. These were the same activities which the parents were asked about (see Chapter 5 above).

Their responses were averaged across the five literacy skills and are presented in Table 6.4, together with the PIRLS reading assessment and the corresponding international averages.

**Table 6.4 Pupils categorised by headteachers' estimate of the percentage beginning school with early literacy skills**

| More than 75% begin school with skills | | 51–75% begin school with skills | | 25–50% begin school with skills | | Less than 25% begin school with skills | |
|---|---|---|---|---|---|---|---|
| Per cent of pupils | Average achievement | Per cent of pupils | Average achievement | Per cent of pupils | Average achievement | Per cent of pupils | Average achievement |
| 61 | 566 | 19 | 543 | 11 | 533 | 9 | 548 |
| (14) | (500) | (12) | (511) | (19) | (506) | (55) | (493) |

Data available for 70–84 per cent of pupils; (international average)

Only Singapore (63 per cent) reported that a higher percentage of their pupils began school with more than three-quarters of them possessing the five specified literacy skills. Slovenia, like England, reported that 61 per cent of their pupils were in schools where the headteachers reported that more than three-quarters of beginning pupils possessed a range of literacy skills.

Table 6.5 provides further detail of headteachers' estimates of the reading readiness of their pupils when they begin school (year 1 in England) by showing the percentage of year 5 pupils in schools where the headteacher reported that more than three-quarters of beginning pupils had specific early literacy skills. International averages are also given.

**Table 6.5 Pupils in schools where headteachers estimate that more than 75 per cent begin school with specific early literacy skills**

| Percentage of pupils attending such schools | | | | |
|---|---|---|---|---|
| Recognise most of the alphabet | Write letters of the alphabet | Read some words | Write some words | Read sentences |
| 58 | 55 | 64 | 44 | 29 |
| (24) | (19) | (17) | (14) | (10) |

Data available for 70–84 per cent of pupils; (international average)

Across all five literacy skills, the figures recorded for England were significantly higher than the corresponding international average. Only Singapore, Slovenia and the United States had higher percentages than England for recognising most of the alphabet (78, 73 and 61 per cent), and writing letters of the alphabet (69, 66, and 56 per cent). Only Singapore, Slovenia and Hong Kong had higher percentages than England for writing some words (51, 59 and 92 per cent) and reading sentences (39, 51 and 86 per cent). Hong Kong alone had a higher percentage for reading some words (93 per cent). High achieving countries such as Sweden, The Netherlands and Bulgaria have much lower percentages of children entering school with high levels of literacy skills. There is no clear relationship between headteachers' estimates of the early literacy skills of their new entrants and a country's overall reading achievement as measured by PIRLS.

## 6.3    The teaching of reading

Chapter 4 of this report outlined some of the current features of the teaching and assessment of reading in England. The National Curriculum and national literacy strategy provide a framework within which much of the literacy instruction is situated. The PIRLS survey included questions about the teaching of reading that were applicable in an international context, in order to facilitate comparisons between countries. In addition to this, the England survey posed some specific questions about the national literacy strategy.

### Background factors

In England, as in most countries in the PIRLS survey, the year 5 curriculum was heavily influenced by external factors. On average internationally, 80 per cent of pupils attended schools where the headteacher reported that the national or regional curriculum had a lot of influence. In England the figure was 92 per cent. National or regional examinations or assessments of pupil achievement had an important influence on the school curriculum in several countries. In England 59 per cent of the pupils attended schools where the headteacher reported they had such influence compared to an international average of 28 per cent. This finding confirms the relative importance of national tests within the English school system. Singapore (97 per cent), Scotland (68 per cent), and the United States (63 per cent) had higher proportions and Moldova the same as England.

Headteachers in England reported much higher levels of co-ordination and whole-school initiatives concerned with the teaching of reading than the average internationally.

The overall average class size in England was 29 against the international average of 26, although the teachers reported that 43 per cent of the pupils in England were taught in classes of 31 or more pupils compared with the international average of 23 per cent. The relationship internationally between class size and reading achievement is difficult to interpret and is complicated by the fact that small classes are sometimes used both for pupils with special educational needs and for high attaining pupils.

### Teaching time

The pupils in the England sample had 958 hours of instructional time per year against an international average of 837 hours. An estimated 29 per cent of the time in England was spent on language work (32 per cent internationally) and 15 per cent on reading (24 per cent internationally). Teachers in England estimated that they spent an average of 7 hours a week on language teaching, which was the same as the international average. They estimated that they spent an average of 4 hours each week on both formal reading teaching and informal reading activities across the curriculum, which was one hour less than the international average. Table 6.6 shows the reported frequency of reading teaching during the week, together with the associated PIRLS reading achievement scores.

**Table 6.6   Frequency of reading teaching during the week**

| Every day | | 3–4 days a week | | Fewer than 3 days a week | |
|---|---|---|---|---|---|
| Per cent of pupils | Average achievement | Per cent of pupils | Average achievement | Per cent of pupils | Average achievement |
| 74 | 551 | 23 | 564 | 3 | 570 |
| (54) | (500) | (35) | (500) | (10) | (495) |

Data: Teachers' questionnaire; (international average)

According to the teachers' reports, 74 per cent of pupils are taught reading on a daily basis. There is no association between the frequency of reading teaching during the week and pupils' achievement on the PIRLS reading assessment.

To investigate how often pupils read independently, an index was constructed of responses to two questions – how frequently pupils read silently on their own and how frequently they read books of their own choosing. Table 6.7 gives a summary of this index.

**Table 6.7  Pupils' reports of independent reading**

| Every day or almost every day | | Once or twice a week | | Once or twice begin school | | Never or almost begin school | |
|---|---|---|---|---|---|---|---|
| Per cent of pupils | Average achievement | Per cent of pupils | Average achievement | Per cent of pupils | Average achievement | Per cent of pupils | Average achievement |
| 83 | 558 | 14 | 535 | 1 | ~ | 1 | ~ |
| (66) | (507) | (27) | (494) | (4) | (474) | (3) | (459) |

N = 3156; (international average)

~ Insufficient data to report achievement

In just two countries, New Zealand (86 per cent) and the United States (84 per cent), a greater proportion of pupils reported more frequent independent reading. In England, as in the majority of countries, there was a positive association between the frequency of opportunities to read independently and reading achievement.

## Teaching programmes and class organisation

Unlike the majority of countries in the PIRLS survey, the majority of pupils in the England sample (63 per cent) were in schools where pupils at different reading levels followed different programmes for the teaching of reading. New Zealand (82 per cent) and Iceland (70 per cent) exceeded the figures for England. Only 29 per cent of pupils in the international sample were in schools which followed this practice. The majority of pupils internationally, 60 per cent compared to 37 per cent for England, attended schools which followed the same teaching programmes but at different speeds. Using the same teaching programme at the same speed was used in schools attended by 11 per cent of the pupils internationally. Two countries, England and Iceland, never used this method.

In England, teachers reported that the majority (60 per cent) of pupils were taught using a variety of grouping arrangements. The international average for using a variety of organisational approaches was 46 per cent of pupils being taught in such classes. For 25 per cent of the pupils in England (38 per cent internationally), reading was most commonly taught as a whole class activity. For 27 per cent of pupils, it was most commonly taught in same ability groups (nine per cent internationally).

The preferred approach in England (48 per cent) was to combine the teaching of language as a separate subject with doing reading or language activities as part of teaching other curriculum areas. This was also the preferred approach internationally (58 per cent). For 43 per cent of the pupils in England, reading was taught as a separate subject, compared to 20 per cent internationally.

Headteachers were asked to report on the types of materials used as a basis for their schools' teaching programmes. The results are shown in Table 6.8. (Categories are not mutually exclusive.)

**Table 6.8  Materials used as a basis for reading programmes**

| Percentage of pupils attending schools that used as a basis: | | | | |
|---|---|---|---|---|
| reading schemes | textbooks | variety of children's books | children's newspapers or magazines | materials from different curricular areas |
| 53 | 28 | 48 | 5 | 21 |
| (49) | (75) | (15) | (5) | (13) |

Data: Headteachers' questionnaire; (international average)

In England, 53 per cent of pupils attended schools that use reading schemes (49 per cent internationally) and 28 per cent attended schools that use textbooks (75 per cent internationally). England recorded the highest use of a variety of children's books with 48 per cent of pupils in schools that use them as a basis for the teaching of reading, similar to that reported in France (46 per cent) and substantially higher than that reported by Bulgaria (5 per cent), New Zealand (33 per cent), The Netherlands (19 per cent) and Sweden (36 per cent). Headteachers in England reported the third lowest use of textbooks (28 per cent), behind Greece (4 per cent) and New Zealand (8 per cent).

An interesting contrast can be made with the data from Scotland where 95 per cent of pupils are taught by schools where reading schemes form the basis of the reading programme and 16 per cent are in schools where a variety of children's books are used. Over half (56 per cent) are in schools where textbooks form the basis.

Teachers were asked about the frequency with which they used different types of materials in their teaching. Responses for specific text types were combined to form an index. The results are shown in Table 6.9.

**Table 6.9   Teachers' use of fiction and non-fiction texts in the teaching of reading**

| Percentage of pupils whose teachers asked them to read | | | | | | | |
|---|---|---|---|---|---|---|---|
| Fiction | | | | Non-fiction | | | |
| At least weekly | | Less than weekly | | At least weekly | | Less than weekly | |
| Per cent of pupils | Average achievement | Per cent of pupils | Average achievement | Per cent of pupils | Average achievement | Per cent of pupils | Average achievement |
| 80 | 554 | 20 | 554 | 56 | 552 | 44 | 557 |
| (84) | (501) | (16) | (495) | (55) | (501) | (44) | (501) |

Data available for 70–84 per cent of pupils; (international average)

The results for England are very similar to the international average and show the emphasis on fiction in the teaching of reading to this age group. In just one country (Argentina) were pupils more frequently asked to read non-fiction than fiction.

Table 6.10 presents information about the types of children's books used.

**Table 6.10   Types of fiction used for teaching reading**

| Percentage of pupils whose teachers asked them to read at least weekly: | | | | |
|---|---|---|---|---|
| fables and fairy tales | stories | longer books with chapters | poems | plays |
| 11 | 72 | 56 | 29 | 12 |
| (45) | (65) | (31) | (41) | (8) |

Data: Teachers' questionnaire; (international average)

Teachers in England were more likely to use stories and longer books with chapters than their international counterparts and less likely to use fables, fairy tales and poems.

Table 6.11 presents teachers' reports about how often they used a textbook or a reading series in the teaching of reading and how often they used workbooks and worksheets.

**Table 6.11   Teachers' use of textbooks/reading schemes and workbooks/worksheets**

| Percentage of pupils whose teachers used: | | | | | | | |
|---|---|---|---|---|---|---|---|
| textbooks or reading schemes | | | workbooks or worksheets | | | both textbooks and worksheets daily | textbooks daily and workbooks at least weekly |
| Daily | Weekly | 1–2 times a month or less | Daily | Weekly | 1–2 times a month or less | | |
| 43 | 41 | 16 | 23 | 57 | 20 | 14 | 37 |
| (68) | (24) | (8) | (32) | (46) | (22) | (25) | (53) |

Data: Teachers' questionnaire; (international average)

On average, over 80 per cent of pupils in England had daily or weekly teaching based on a textbook or reading scheme.

## National literacy strategy

Teachers in England were asked questions specifically about the national literacy strategy. Sixty-three per cent of them reported that their pupils received four or more guided reading sessions each month and a further 15 per cent that they received three sessions each month. Table 6.12 shows what the teachers did during those guided reading sessions.

**Table 6.12   What teachers do in a guided reading session**

| Activity | Per cent of pupils whose teachers reported the activity |
|---|---|
| Ask pupils to read aloud around the group | 84 |
| Ask pupils to read to themselves at their own pace | 68 |
| Listen to individual pupils read | 72 |
| Prepare the pupils for particularly difficult parts of the text | 75 |
| Discuss strategies the pupils can use when they get stuck on a word | 94 |
| Help the pupils to use strategies such as skimming and scanning | 89 |
| Help the pupils to use inference and deduction | 91 |

Data: Teachers' questionnaire

It can be seen that there is a high level of consistency in what the teachers do during the guided reading sessions.

When asked about the range of texts used, 84 per cent of the teachers in the survey in 2001 thought they covered a wider range of reading texts with their pupils than they had three years ago.

In September 2000, the national literacy strategy resource book and training video was sent to all schools, and LEAs organised training sessions based on them.  Teachers were asked how useful they found those resources.  Eighty per cent found the 'Grammar for Writing' book either useful or very useful, 61 per cent found the associated training video useful or very useful, and 74 per cent found the LEA training either useful or very useful.

## Reading resources

Since access to books and other print resources is such an important support for the process of learning to read, PIRLS asked headteachers if their schools had a library or reading corners.  Within the PIRLS survey, 91 per cent of pupils in England were in a school where all or most classes had their own library compared with an international average of 57 per cent.  Teachers in England with classroom libraries reported that they allowed their pupils to use those libraries daily in 57 per cent of the cases (37 per cent internationally).  The average number of books with different titles in the classroom were 211 in England and 60 internationally.  Just Canada (250) and the United States (219) had higher mean numbers of

nfer

books. School libraries of more than 500 books were available to 84 per cent of the pupils in the schools in the England survey compared to 65 per cent internationally.

Another reading resource is the availability of specialist staff in addition to the classroom teacher. In England, 13 per cent of pupils were in classrooms where learning or special needs support was always available and 64 per cent were in classes where it was sometimes available. This is similar to the situation in Scotland and Sweden but different to that in The Netherlands where teachers of 41 per cent of pupils reported that a reading specialist was always available.

## Reading as homework

PIRLS created an index of reading for homework based on how often teachers assigned reading as part of homework and how much time they expected pupils to spend on homework involving reading (in any subject). A high level on the index indicates those pupils who are expected to spend more than 30 minutes at least 1–2 times a week. A low level on the index indicates pupils who are never assigned homework or are expected to spend no more than 30 minutes less than once a week. Medium level indicates all other combinations of frequencies. The index is shown as Table 6.13.

**Table 6.13   Index of reading for homework**

| High | | Medium | | Low | |
|---|---|---|---|---|---|
| Per cent of pupils | Average achievement | Per cent of pupils | Average achievement | Per cent of pupils | Average achievement |
| 25 | 554 | 61 | 554 | 13 | 565 |
| (44) | (501) | (46) | (501) | (10) | (490) |

Data: Teachers' questionnaire; (international average)

Pupils in England are likely to receive reading homework less frequently than their international peers. There is no observable relationship between reading homework, as measured by the index, and reading achievement both within and between countries.

## 6.4    Use of computers

Over half of pupils in England were in schools where headteachers reported fewer than five year 5 pupils to each computer. This was considerably greater provision than the international average and is reported in Table 6.14.

**Table 6.14    Headteachers' reports of number of year 5 (4th grade) pupils per computer**

| Fewer than 5 pupils | | 5–10 pupils | | 11–20 pupils | | More than 20 pupils | | Pupils in schools without any computers | |
|---|---|---|---|---|---|---|---|---|---|
| Per cent of pupils | Average achievement | Per cent of pupils | Average achievement | Per cent of pupils | Average achievement | Per cent of pupils | Average achievement | Per cent of pupils | Average achievement |
| 59 | 559 | 24 | 553 | 13 | 551 | 2 | 541 | 0 | – |
| (30) | (528) | (22) | (522) | (10) | (523) | (7) | (515) | (31) | (499) |

Data: Headteachers' questionnaire; (international average)

Headteachers were also asked about Internet access of computers used by year 5 (4th grade) pupils and this is shown in Table 6.15.

**Table 6.15    Proportion of computers with access to the Internet**

| All | | Most | | Some | | None | |
|---|---|---|---|---|---|---|---|
| Per cent of pupils | Average achievement | Per cent of pupils | Average achievement | Per cent of pupils | Average achievement | Per cent of pupils | Average achievement |
| 40 | 553 | 33 | 554 | 14 | 548 | 12 | 558 |
| (26) | (528) | (8) | (531) | (12) | (523) | (54) | (504) |

Data: Headteachers' questionnaire; (international average)

Forty per cent of pupils in England were in schools where all the computers had access to the Internet, more than the international average. Internationally, over half of the pupils do not have access at school to computers connected to the Internet. There was no clear association between the proportion of computers with access to the Internet and reading achievement.

Teachers were asked about the availability of computers for use by their class and this is shown in Table 6.16.

**Table 6.16    Computer availability for use by class**

| Percentage of pupils whose teachers reported | | | |
|---|---|---|---|
| Computers available: | | | Computers not available |
| in classroom | elsewhere in school | have Internet access | |
| 88 | 95 | 86 | 1 |
| (29) | (45) | (36) | (50) |

Data available for 70–84 per cent of pupils; (international average)

As with data provided by headteachers, pupils in England had much greater access to computers and to the Internet than children in most other countries.

Teachers were also asked about the literacy activities undertaken on the computer by their pupils and this is reported in Table 6.17.

**Table 6.17   Use of computers for teaching purposes**

| Percentage of pupils whose teachers reported using computers for teaching purposes at least monthly | | |
|---|---|---|
| Pupils read stories or other texts on the computer | Pupils use educational software to develop reading skills and strategies | Pupils write stories or other texts on the computer |
| 56 | 55 | 93 |
| (22) | (21) | (32) |

Data: Teachers' questionnaire; (international average)

Further information about computer use was provided by the pupils and this is shown in Table 6.18.

**Table 6.18   Pupils' reports of computer use**

| Percentage of pupils who reported ever using a computer | Percentage of pupils who reported using a computer at least weekly | | |
|---|---|---|---|
| | At home | At school | At some other place |
| 97 | 74 | 67 | 29 |
| (70) | (46) | (29) | (23) |

Data: Pupils' questionnaire; (international average)

Children in England are much more likely to use computers at home and school than the average for all children in PIRLS.

Overall, pupils and teachers in England reported considerably greater computer use, including access to the Internet.  Other countries recording a high level of computer access and use included Canada, Iceland, The Netherlands, New Zealand, Scotland, Singapore, Sweden and the United States.

## 6.5   Home–school involvement

To measure the extent of home–school communication, PIRLS created an index based on schools' average response to six questions about the opportunities for parental involvement provided by the school and about parental attendance at school-sponsored meetings or other events.  Pupils were placed in the high category if schools held parent–teacher conferences and other events at school to which parents were invited, and more than half attended, four or more times a year; schools sent home letters, calendars and newsletters with information about the school seven or more times a year; and they sent written reports, or report cards, of pupils' performance four or more times a year. The low category indicates that schools never held parent–teacher conferences, or if conferences were held, fewer than one quarter of the parents attended; schools sent home letters, calendars or newsletters about the school three times a year or fewer; and they sent home written reports of children's performance once a year or less. The medium category indicates all other combinations of parental involvement opportunities and participation. Table 6.19 presents a summary of this index.

**Table 6.19   Index of home–school involvement**

| High | | Medium | | Low | |
|---|---|---|---|---|---|
| Per cent of pupils | Average achievement | Per cent of pupils | Average achievement | Per cent of pupils | Average achievement |
| 15 | 577 | 71 | 551 | 14 | 544 |
| (41) | (508) | (28) | (499) | (31) | (490) |

(International average)

The Netherlands had the third highest percentage of pupils in the high category (92 per cent) behind the United States (97 per cent) and Canada (96 per cent). Sweden had 33 per cent of pupils in that category, below the international average of 41 per cent. Only 15 per cent of pupils in England attended schools in the high category of the index of home–school involvement. One country, Moldova, had the same percentage of pupils in that category as England and four countries in the survey had fewer pupils in that category: Macedonia (10 per cent), Turkey (8 per cent), Bulgaria (8 per cent) and Morocco (7 per cent). However, 86 per cent of pupils in England were in schools in the medium or high categories against an international average of 69 per cent. It should be noted that the index did not include less formal means of communication between home and school and, in the case of England, probably reflects the custom in many schools of frequent but less formal contact between home and school.

Another measure of home–school communication concerns the frequency with which the pupils' teachers reported they sent classroom work in language home. Table 6.20 shows that teachers of 62 per cent of the pupils internationally sent home examples of the pupils' classroom work in language at least monthly. For England the equivalent figure is 13 per cent.

**Table 6.20   Teachers send home examples of pupils' classroom work in language**

| Weekly | | Monthly | | Six times a year or less | |
|---|---|---|---|---|---|
| Per cent of pupils | Average achievement | Per cent of pupils | Average achievement | Per cent of pupils | Average achievement |
| 7 | 583 | 6 | 546 | 86 | 552 |
| (31) | (506) | (31) | (498) | (38) | (495) |

Data: Teachers' questionnaire; (international average)

PIRLS also collected data from parents on how often their child's school asked them to make sure the child did their language homework, how often they were given or sent home examples of classroom work in language, and how often they were given or sent home information about the child's performance in language. This is reported in Table 6.21.

**Table 6.21   Schools ask parents to review pupils' language progress**

| Often | | Sometimes | | Never or almost never | |
|---|---|---|---|---|---|
| Per cent of pupils | Average achievement | Per cent of pupils | Average achievement | Per cent of pupils | Average achievement |
| 36 | 572 | 21 | 575 | 44 | 569 |
| (48) | (504) | (20) | (504) | (32) | (513) |

Data: Home questionnaire; (international average)

Table 6.21 shows the average for the parent responses to those questions and demonstrates that, once again within the measure of home–school communication, there was a lower percentage of pupils for England in the highest category than the international average. There is no observable relationship between this index and performance on the PIRLS reading assessment.

The parents of about half (49 per cent) of pupils in PIRLS in England agreed a lot with the statement that their child's school made an effort to include them in their child's education, a figure only slightly below the international average of 52 per cent. In England, the proportion of pupils whose parents who agreed a lot that the school cared about their child's progress (68 per cent) was slightly above the international average (66 per cent). The proportion of pupils whose parents agreed a lot that the school did a good job in helping their child to read (59 per cent) was slightly below the international average (64 per cent).

It can be seen from this data that even though the measures used in PIRLS place schools in England at the lower end of the index of home–school involvement, parents are not significantly less satisfied with the level of contact with their children's schools than the international average.

# 7. Other Factors Associated with Reading Achievement

---

**This chapter looks at the impact of different background factors on reading achievement, and reading attitudes and activities.**

---

- When all other factors are controlled, girls scored more highly than boys in the PIRLS assessments in England. Older pupils tended to score more highly, as did pupils born in the UK. Children with more books in the home, those who are more positive about reading and the more confident readers tended to have higher scores, whereas those from larger families and those who reported doing more reading activities at home and at school, tended to have lower scores.

- Girls, children born in the UK and those from smaller families, tended to be more positive and confident about reading.

- Girls, children in schools where the headteacher reported higher levels of disadvantage, and children who were born outside the UK, tended to be involved in more reading activities at home and at school.

- Boys tended to report higher levels of television viewing than girls, as did children born in the UK and those from smaller families.

- Children with more books at home tended to be higher achieving, to be more positive and confident about reading, to participate in reading activities at home more frequently, to talk more about their reading and to make more use of computers.

Previous chapters have reported some notable findings from the study, generally where a particular aspect or factor is associated with a higher, or lower, score or sometimes where there is no apparent association when one might have been expected. Some clear patterns have emerged from the international data – the superior performance of girls, for example, whereas other findings are of more local interest – children in rural schools in England tended to score more highly than those in suburban or urban schools, for example.

The analysis in this chapter attempts to take into account ('control for') all the things ('background variables') which might influence what is being measured. For example, taking into account factors such as school size and location, pupils' age and sex, how much influence does the proportion of pupils eligible for free school meals in a school have on

PIRLS achievement scores? The statistical technique used is known as multilevel modelling, but its use will not be described here. Rather, the results of the analysis will be presented.

In addition to looking at the impact of specific factors on achievement, seven other scales were identified by carrying out an exploratory factor analysis of pupil questionnaire data. This is an attempt to group together data from items in the questionnaires which are highly correlated and therefore can assumed to be measuring the same construct. These scales are shown below; the questionnaire items included in each scale are listed in Appendix 2.

- pupil attitude scales
  - reading enjoyment
  - reading confidence
- pupil activity scales
  - reading activities in class
  - reading activities at home
  - use of computers
  - talking about reading
  - television viewing habits

The variables analysed also included background information at school and pupil level, such as the percentage of pupils eligible for free school meals (school level) and the size of the family (pupil level). The variables included are listed in Appendix 2.

The estimated relationships with the achievement scales and the background variables have been converted into 'normalised coefficients' which represent the strength of each relationship as a percentage. This allows for a comparision of the apparent influence of different variables on the outcome, when all other variables are controlled.

These have been coded in the tables below.

**Positive relationships (associated with higher results)**

| Small | Medium | Large |
|---|---|---|
| ⇑ 1% to 10% | ⇑ ⇑ 11% to 20% | ⇑ ⇑ ⇑ more than +20% |

**Negative relationships (associated with lower results)**

| Small | Medium | Large |
|---|---|---|
| ⇓ −1% to −10% | ⇓ ⇓ −11% to −20% | ⇓ ⇓ ⇓ less than −20% |

## Relationships with background factors

For each scale, the significant relationships (those which are unlikely to have occurred by chance) with background factors (controlling for all other factors) are shown in the figures and summarised below.

### Achievement scales: overall, literary and information scores

Figure 7.1 shows the impact of the background factors on the overall reading achievement score and for literary and informational reading separately.

**Figure 7.1   Summary of results for achievement scores (significant normalised coefficients)**

(Significant coefficients at 5% level)

| Variable | Total score | Literary score | Information score |
|---|---|---|---|
| Sex (0 = male, 1 = female) | ⇑ | ⇑ | |
| Age in years at testing | ⇑ | ⇑ | ⇑ |
| English as an additional language | ⇓ | | ⇓ |
| Born outside UK | ⇓⇓ | ⇓⇓ | ⇓⇓ |
| Number of books in the home | ⇑⇑ | ⇑⇑ | ⇑ |
| Number of children at home | ⇓ | ⇓ | ⇓ |
| Attitude factor: reading enjoyment | ⇑⇑⇑ | ⇑⇑⇑ | ⇑⇑⇑ |
| Attitude factor: reading confidence | ⇑⇑⇑ | ⇑⇑⇑ | ⇑⇑⇑ |
| Activity factor: reading activities in class | ⇓ | ⇓ | ⇓ |
| Activity factor: reading activities at home | ⇓⇓ | ⇓⇓ | ⇓⇓ |
| Activity factor: talking about reading | | | |
| Activity factor: use of computers | ⇓ | ⇓ | |
| Activity factor: TV viewing habits | ⇑ | ⇑ | ⇑ |
| Rural school location | | | |
| Suburban school location | | | |
| Number of year 5 in cohort | | | |
| Percentage eligible for free school meals | ⇓⇓ | | ⇓⇓ |
| KS1 test results overall 1998 (5 pt scale) | | | |
| School background: headteacher's estimate of attainment on entry to year 1 | | | |
| School background: headteacher's estimate of disadvantage | | | |

The figure shows that even when all other variables are controlled, girls scored more highly than boys overall and on both the literary and information scales, although the latter is not a significant difference.  Older pupils tended to have higher scores on all three scales, confirming other evidence of a season of birth effect, where summer born children have tended to score less well on various measures of achievement.

Pupils born in the UK tended to have higher scores on all three scales, whilst children with English as an additional language tended to have lower overall and information scores.

Even when other aspects such as gender are controlled, children with more books in the home, those who reported higher levels of reading enjoyment and of reading confidence, tended to have higher scores on all three scales, whereas children in larger families, those who reported doing more reading activities at home and at school tended to have lower scores.

With respect to other activities, pupils who reported more use of computers tended to have lower overall reading scores and specifically lower literary scores, whilst those reporting higher levels of television viewing also recorded higher achievement scores. The factor analysis indicated a correlation between frequency of television viewing and also duration. However, the relationship between reading achievement in PIRLS and television viewing habits is clearly a complex one and requires further investigation.

Pupils in schools with higher percentages of children eligible for free school meals tended to have lower scores on all three scales (but this was significant only at the 10 per cent level for the literary scale).

## Pupil attitude scales: reading enjoyment and reading confidence

Figure 7.2 shows the impact of the background factors on the reading enjoyment and confidence scales.

**Figure 7.2   Summary of results for attitude factors (significant normalised coefficients)**

(Significant coefficients at 5% level)

| Variable | Attitude factor: reading enjoyment | Attitude factor: reading confidence |
|---|---|---|
| Sex (0 = male, 1 = female) | ⇧ ⇧ ⇧ | ⇧ |
| Age in years at testing | | |
| English as an additional language | | |
| Born outside UK | ⇩ | ⇩ |
| Number of books in the home | ⇧ ⇧ ⇧ | ⇧ ⇧ |
| Number of children at home | ⇩ | ⇩ |
| Rural school location | | |
| Suburban school location | | |
| Number of year 5 in cohort | | |
| Percentage eligible for free school meals | | |
| KS1 test results overall 1998 (5 pt scale) | | |
| School background: headteacher's estimate of attainment on entry to year 1 | ⇧ | |
| School background: headteacher's estimate of disadvantage | ⇧ | |

Higher scores on the reading enjoyment scale were associated with higher achievement scores (as reported in section 5.1 above), but even when the higher performance of girls was controlled for they tended to score more highly on the reading enjoyment scale in PIRLS (see Figure 7.2). Girls also scored more highly on the reading confidence scale, although gender had less effect than on the enjoyment scale. Pupils born in the UK tended to have higher scores.

Children reporting more books at home tended to have higher scores, as did pupils with fewer siblings.

Pupils in schools where headteachers reported higher skills on entry to year 1 and also those in schools where headteachers estimated higher levels of disadvantage amongst the pupils tended to score more highly on the reading enjoyment scale.

### Pupil activity scales: reading activities at home and school and talking about reading / use of computers and TV viewing habits

Figure 7.3 shows the impact of the background factors on the reading activities at school and at home scales, and the scales concerned with talking about reading, the use of computers and television viewing.

**Figure 7.3   Summary of results for activity factors (significant normalised coefficients)**

(Significant coefficients at 5% level)

| Variable | Reading activities: school | Reading activities: home | Talking about reading | Use of computers | TV viewing habits |
|---|---|---|---|---|---|
| Sex (0 = male, 1 = female) | ⇧ ⇧ | ⇧ ⇧ | ⇧ ⇧ ⇧ | | ⇩ |
| Age in years at testing | | | | | ⇧ |
| English as an additional language | | | | | |
| Born outside UK | ⇧ | ⇧ | | ⇧ | ⇩ |
| Number of books in the home | | ⇧ | ⇧ ⇧ | ⇧ ⇧ | |
| Number of children at home | ⇧ | | | ⇧ | ⇩ |
| Rural school location | | | | | |
| Suburban school location | | | | | |
| Number of year 5 in cohort | | | | | |
| Percentage eligible for free school meals | | | | | |
| KS1 test results overall 1998 (5 pt scale) | | | | | |
| School background: headteacher's estimate of attainment on entry to year 1 | | | ⇧ | | |
| School background: headteacher's estimate of disadvantage | ⇧ ⇧ ⇧ | ⇧ ⇧ | ⇧ ⇧ | ⇧ | |

This figure shows an interesting effect of gender on the reading activities at home and school scale. Higher scores on this scale were associated with lower attainment, but once gender had been controlled for, girls tended to report carrying out more reading activities at home, and talking more about reading.

Children who have more books in the home tended to engage in more reading activities at home and to talk more about their reading at home.

Pupils in schools in which headteachers estimated higher levels of disadvantage tended to engage in more reading activities both at home and at school and also to talk more about their reading at home. There was, though, no association between the reporting of home and school reading activities and the percentage of children eligible for free school meals.

In this analysis, when other factors are controlled, there is a positive association between boys and television viewing (duration and frequency).

When other factors were controlled, pupils born outside the UK and those in larger families reported greater use of computers whilst watching television less often and for shorter periods. Children in schools where headteachers estimated greater levels of disadvantage reported greater computer usage, but there was no clear association between the percentage of children eligible for free school meals and reported use of computers or television viewing habits.

# Appendix 1: Sampling in PIRLS 2001

## A1.1 Principles

### Defining the population

The target population for PIRLS 2001 ('the international desired target population') was defined as:

*All students enrolled in the upper of the two adjacent grades that contain the largest proportion of 9-year-olds at the time of testing.*

This was year 5 in England. Year 5 was therefore described as the 'national desired population'. In the definition of the sampling frame (the 'national defined population'), schools that were extremely small were excluded, as were special schools. These amounted to 1.83% of the target population. These exclusions were approved by Statistics Canada which drew the national school sample for England.

### Within-school exclusions

Each country had to define its own within-school exclusions. These were limited to pupils for whom the PIRLS tests were inappropriate and the definition adopted in each country had to be approved by the International Study Center at Boston College and by Statistics Canada. In England, within-school exclusions were defined as follows:

*Pupils with functional disabilities such as physical or sensory impairment*

- Has a permanent physical disability (eg a lack of fine motor control) or sensory impairment (eg visual or auditory impairment) which would mean they were unable to participate in the PIRLS testing situation.

*Other pupils with special educational needs*

- Has a statement of special educational needs, other than those described above.

- Has been referred for multiprofessional assessment.

- Is temporarily unable to cope with the test conditions (eg a child with epilepsy who has had a fit earlier in the day and is consequently unable to concentrate).

*Children who are learning English as an additional language*

- Pupils for whom English is not their first language who have been taught in English for less than one year

- Pupils for whom English is not their first language who, in the professional opinion of their teachers, despite having received a year's education in English, still lack fluency in reading and writing in the English language. In practice, this could apply to:
  - pupils who still receive additional English language support from a teacher who has responsibility for supporting pupils who use English as an additional language;
  - pupils whose class teacher regularly provides specific English language support within lessons to enable those pupils to carry out learning activities.

## Sample design

PIRLS 2001 used a two-stage stratification cluster sample design. The first stage consisted of identifying a sample of schools. The second stage was the identification of one classroom from the target year group in each sampled school.

In PIRLS, pupils are the principal units of analysis but findings are reported on school, teacher and classroom characteristics. In order to ensure that there was a sufficiently large sample of schools and classrooms, a sample of 150 schools was drawn from the target population.

The samples for England (main, first and second replacement) were drawn and checked by Statistics Canada in consultation with the NFER.

### Stratification

Explicit stratification: this is the construction of separate sampling frames for each stratification variable. In England, there was explicit stratification by school size (large/small) ensuring disproportionate allocation of the school sample across the two strata with schools in the 'small schools' stratum sampled with equal probabilities.

Implicit stratification: this requires a single school-sampling frame but sorts the schools in this frame by a set of stratification variables. It is intended to ensure proportional sample allocation. In England, the implicit stratification variables were school type (primary, junior/middle, independent) and school performance (1998 key stage 2 performance, six levels).

### Replacement schools

Not all schools sampled in England are willing to participate in PIRLS. In order to maintain sample numbers, a main sample and two parallel samples were drawn. For each school drawn, the next school on the ordered sample frame was identified as its replacement and the next one as a second replacement. This ensured that first and second replacement schools had the same characteristics (as identified in the stratification) as the sampled school. PIRLS had a target of a minimum response rate of 85% of sampled schools (see section A1.2).

### First sampling stage

PIRLS used a systematic probability-proportional-to-size (PPS) technique to identify schools. This requires a measure of size (MOS) for each school, in this case the number of year 5 pupils enrolled in the school. The effect of PPS is to ensure that larger schools are more likely to be selected than smaller schools and that schools of equal size have an equal probability of being selected.

### Second sampling stage

One class per school was sampled. All classes were selected with equal probability.

## A1.2 Participation rates

PIRLS identifies three categories of sampling participation.

| Category 1 | Acceptable sampling participation rate **without** the use of replacement schools. In order to be placed in this category, a country had to have:<br><br>● An **unweighted** school response rate **without** replacement of at least 85% (after rounding to the nearest whole per cent) AND an **unweighted** student response rate (after rounding) of at least 85%.<br><br>OR<br><br>● A **weighted** school response rate **without** replacement of at least 85% (after rounding to the nearest whole per cent) AND a **weighted** student response rate (after rounding) of at least 85%.<br><br>OR<br><br>● The product of the (unrounded) **weighted** school response rate **without** replacement and the (unrounded) **weighted** student response rate of at least 75% (after rounding to the nearest whole per cent).<br><br>Countries in this category appeared in the tables and figures in international reports without annotation ordered by achievement as appropriate. |
|---|---|
| Category 2 | Acceptable sampling participation rate **only when replacement schools were included**.<br><br>A country was placed in category 2 if:<br><br>● It failed to meet the requirements for Category 1 but had either an **unweighted** or **weighted** school response rate **without** replacement of at least 50% (after rounding to the nearest whole per cent).<br><br>AND HAD<br><br>● An **unweighted** school response rate **with** replacement of at least 85% (after rounding to the nearest whole per cent) AND an **unweighted** student response rate (after rounding) of at least 85%.<br><br>OR<br><br>● A **weighted** school response rate **with** replacement of at least 85% (after rounding to nearest whole per cent) AND a **weighted** student response rate (after rounding) of at least 85%.<br><br>OR<br><br>● The product of the (unrounded) **weighted** school response rate **with** replacement and the (unrounded) **weighted** student response rate of at least 75% (after rounding to the nearest whole per cent).<br><br>Countries in this category were annotated in the tables and figures in international reports and ordered by achievement as appropriate. |
| Category 3 | Unacceptable sampling response rate even when replacement schools are included. Countries that could provide documentation to show that they complied with PIRLS sampling procedures and requirements but did not meet the requirements for Category 1 or Category 2 were placed in Category 3.<br><br>Countries in this category would appear in a separate section of the achievement tables, below the other countries, in international reports. These countries would be presented in alphabetical order. |

Foy and Joncas (2002)

**Table A1.1  Allocation of school sample in England**

| Explicit stratum | Total sampled schools | Ineligible schools | Participating schools | | | Non-participating schools |
|---|---|---|---|---|---|---|
| | | | Sampled | 1st replacement | 2nd replacement | |
| Small schools | 25 | 0 | 14 | 9 | 0 | 2 |
| Large schools | 125 | 0 | 74 | 29 | 5 | 17 |
| **Total** | 150 | 0 | 88 | 38 | 5 | 19 |

**Table A1.2  School participation rates**

| Type | Sampled schools | With 1st replacement schools | With 2nd replacement schools |
|---|---|---|---|
| Unweighted | 58.7% | 84.0% | 87.3% |
| Weighted | 57.4% | 84.0% | 87.5% |

**Table A1.3  Pupil participation status**

| Status | Count |
|---|---|
| Excluded – did not participate | 49 |
| No longer in school/class | 46 |
| Absent | 202 |
| Participated | 3156 |
| Booklet lost | 2 |
| Excluded – did participate | 73 |
| Other | 0 |
| **Total** | 3528 |

**Table A1.4  Overall exclusion rates**

| Type | Rate |
|---|---|
| School sampling frame | 1.83% |
| Within-school sampling frame | 3.85% |
| **Overall** | 5.68% |

**Table A1.5   Weighted pupil participation rates**

| Type | Rate |
|---|---|
| Unweighted | 93.9% |
| Weighted | 94.0% |

**Table A1.6   Overall participation rates**

| Type | Sampled schools | With 1st replacement schools | With 2nd replacement schools |
|---|---|---|---|
| Unweighted | 55.1% | 78.9% | 82.0% |
| Weighted | 53.9% | 78.9% | 82.2% |

England met the sampling requirements for category 2:

a)   The overall participation rate was over 50% without the inclusion of replacement schools (Table A1.6)

AND

b)   the product of the (unrounded) weighted school response rate with replacement schools (Table A1.2) and the (unrounded) weighted pupil response rate (Table A1.5) was at least 75%.

## Response rates to questionnaires

Although no explicit targets were set for the questionnaire response rates, tables in the international report are annotated for countries in which response rates fell below 85%.

**Table A1.7   Questionnaire response rates**

| Questionnaire | Number expected | Number returned completed | Percentage returned completed |
|---|---|---|---|
| Pupil | 3156 | 3147 | 99.7% |
| Teacher | 132 | 125 | 94.7% |
| Headteacher | 131 | 124 | 94.7% |
| Parent/guardian | 3156 | 1733 | 54.9% |

## A1.3 Post-survey sampling checks

In addition to the above checks on achieved participation rates, further attempts were made to ascertain the representativeness of the achieved sample at both school and pupil level. The sample representation table for pupils (Table A1.9) shows all year 5 pupils in sampled schools, not just participating pupils.

Significant differences were found between the school population and the achieved sample (Table A1.8) and the pupil population and the achieved sample (Table A1.9) for the variables school type, school size and percentage of pupils eligible for free school meals. These first two significant differences are likely to be due to the probability-proportional-to-size technique adopted with under-representation of small schools. There was over-representation of junior and middle schools at the expense of primary/combined schools. Similarly, there was under-representation of one-form entry schools and an over-representation of larger schools.

On the free school meals variable, there is an under-representation of schools in the lowest quintile of eligibility for free school meals, i.e. the least socially disadvantaged schools. This is probably another result of the under-representation of small schools.

The same analysis was also conducted for the subsample of schools which declined to participate. This gave very similar results to the analysis of participating schools with over-representation of larger schools. In respect of eligibility for free school meals, a greater proportion of declining schools were in the second highest quintile of percentage of pupils eligible whilst those in the lowest quintile were under-represented.

A further comparison was made, this time within the set of schools which were invited to participate between those which agreed to participate and those which declined. On none of the stratification variables identified in Table A1.8 (overleaf) was there a significant difference between these two groups of schools.

nfer

**Table A1.8   Sample representation – schools**

| | Population | | Sampled | | Responded | |
|---|---|---|---|---|---|---|
| | **Number** | **%** | **Number** | **%** | **Number** | **%** |
| **School type** | | | | | | |
| Infant/First | 102 | 1 | 3 | 1 | 1 | 1 |
| Primary/Combined | 11364 | 75 | 275 | 61 | 87 | 65 |
| Junior | 1985 | 13 | 111 | 25 | 29 | 22 |
| Middle | 475 | 3 | 29 | 6 | 10 | 8 |
| Independent | 1275 | 8 | 27 | 6 | 6 | 5 |
| Not available | | | 8 | 2 | | |
| **Size of year group** | | | | | | |
| 1–30 | 6305 | 41 | 99 | 22 | 32 | 24 |
| 31–60 | 6096 | 40 | 166 | 37 | 48 | 36 |
| 61–90 | 2099 | 14 | 123 | 27 | 38 | 29 |
| 91+ | 701 | 5 | 54 | 12 | 14 | 11 |
| Not available | | | 11 | 2 | 1 | 1 |
| **Type of LEA** | | | | | | |
| Metropolitan | 5209 | 34 | 171 | 38 | 47 | 5 |
| Non-Metropolitan | 9992 | 66 | 274 | 60 | 86 | 65 |
| Not available | | | 8 | 2 | | |
| **Region** | | | | | | |
| North | 4842 | 32 | 122 | 27 | 33 | 25 |
| Midlands | 4618 | 30 | 150 | 33 | 48 | 36 |
| South | 5741 | 38 | 173 | 38 | 52 | 39 |
| **KS2 1998 performance** | | | | | | |
| Lowest 20% | 1993 | 13 | 59 | 13 | 18 | 14 |
| 2nd lowest 20% | 3044 | 20 | 100 | 22 | 31 | 23 |
| Middle 20% | 3116 | 20 | 98 | 22 | 27 | 20 |
| 2nd highest 20% | 3087 | 20 | 92 | 20 | 29 | 22 |
| Highest 20% | 3073 | 20 | 72 | 16 | 22 | 17 |
| Not available | 888 | 6 | 32 | 7 | 6 | 5 |
| **Free school meals % 1999** | | | | | | |
| Lowest 20% | 2801 | 18 | 51 | 11 | 13 | 10 |
| 2nd lowest 20% | 3156 | 21 | 100 | 22 | 33 | 25 |
| Middle 20% | 3030 | 20 | 94 | 21 | 30 | 23 |
| 2nd highest 20% | 3080 | 20 | 98 | 22 | 25 | 19 |
| Highest 20% | 3119 | 21 | 98 | 22 | 30 | 23 |
| Not available | 15 | 0 | 12 | 3 | 2 | 2 |
| **Total schools** | 15201 | 100 | 453 | 100 | 133 | 100 |

**Table A1.9  Sample representation – pupil**

| | Population | | Sampled | | Responded | |
|---|---|---|---|---|---|---|
| | **Number** | **%** | **Number** | **%** | **Number** | **%** |
| **School type** | | | | | | |
| Infant/First | 2863 | 0 | 79 | 0 | 25 | 0 |
| Primary/Combined | 392539 | 63 | 11565 | 47 | 3417 | 49 |
| Junior | 142059 | 23 | 9001 | 36 | 2350 | 34 |
| Middle | 46333 | 7 | 3110 | 13 | 962 | 14 |
| Independent | 34417 | 6 | 972 | 4 | 203 | 3 |
| **Size of year group** | | | | | | |
| 1–30 | 124245 | 20 | 2117 | 9 | 598 | 9 |
| 31–60 | 264544 | 43 | 7410 | 30 | 2070 | 30 |
| 61–90 | 150925 | 24 | 8850 | 36 | 2720 | 39 |
| 91+ | 78497 | 13 | 6350 | 26 | 1569 | 23 |
| **Type of LEA** | | | | | | |
| Metropolitan | 227734 | 37 | 9018 | 36 | 2514 | 36 |
| Non-Metropolitan | 390477 | 63 | 15709 | 64 | 4443 | 64 |
| **Region** | | | | | | |
| North | 182115 | 29 | 5640 | 23 | 1383 | 20 |
| Midlands | 190619 | 31 | 8961 | 36 | 2706 | 39 |
| South | 245477 | 40 | 10126 | 41 | 2868 | 41 |
| **KS2 1998 performance** | | | | | | |
| Lowest 20% | 82782 | 13 | 3156 | 13 | 986 | 14 |
| 2nd lowest 20% | 137531 | 22 | 6177 | 25 | 1793 | 26 |
| Middle 20% | 138559 | 22 | 5849 | 24 | 1551 | 22 |
| 2nd highest 20% | 126822 | 21 | 5276 | 21 | 1466 | 21 |
| Highest 20% | 106543 | 17 | 3544 | 14 | 1022 | 15 |
| Not available | 25974 | 4 | 725 | 3 | 139 | 2 |
| **Free school meals % 1999** | | | | | | |
| Lowest 20% | 80499 | 13 | 1798 | 7 | 401 | 6 |
| 2nd lowest 20% | 125591 | 20 | 6018 | 24 | 1506 | 22 |
| Middle 20% | 134363 | 22 | 5871 | 24 | 1847 | 27 |
| 2nd highest 20% | 141141 | 23 | 5879 | 24 | 1547 | 22 |
| Highest 20% | 136336 | 22 | 5152 | 21 | 1647 | 24 |
| Not available | 281 | 0 | 9 | 0 | 9 | 0 |
| **Total pupils** | 618211 | 100 | 24727 | 100 | 6957 | 100 |

# Appendix 2: Background Factors

**Table A2.1  Background variables in multilevel analysis**

| Background factors | Source |
|---|---|
| gender | pupil questionnaire |
| age | pupil questionnaire |
| English as an additional language | pupil questionnaire |
| born in UK | pupil questionnaire |
| number of books in home | pupil questionnaire |
| number of children in home | pupil questionnaire |
| school location (rural/suburban/urban) | school questionnaire |
| number of year 5 pupils in school | school questionnaire |
| eligibility for free school meals | DfES |
| key stage 1 attainment (5 point scale) | DfES |

**Table A2.2  Pupil factors in multilevel analysis**

| Scales derived from factor analysis | Pupil questionnaire |
|---|---|
| 'reading enjoyment' | • I talk to my family about what I am reading<br>• I read for fun outside school<br>• I read stories or novels<br>• I read silently on my own<br>• Time spent on reading for homework<br>• I read only if I have to<br>• I like talking about books with other people<br>• would be happy if someone gave me a book as a present<br>• I think reading is boring<br>• I enjoy reading |
| 'reading confidence' | • Reading is very easy for me<br>• I do not read as well as other children in my class<br>• When I am reading by myself, I understand almost everything I read |

*(continued on next page)*

**Table A2.2   Pupil factors in multilevel analysis** *contd*

| 'reading activities in class' | • I read aloud to the whole class<br>• I read aloud to a small group of children in my class<br>• I read along silently while other children read aloud<br>• I answer questions in a workbook or on a worksheet about what I have read<br>• I write something about what I have read<br>• I answer questions aloud that my teacher asks about what I have read<br>• I talk to other children about what I have read<br>• I draw pictures or do an art project about what I have read<br>• I act in a play about what I have read<br>• I do a group project with other children in the class about what I have read<br>• I take a written quiz or test about what I have read |
|---|---|
| 'reading activities at home' | • I read aloud to someone at home<br>• I listen to someone at home read aloud to me<br>• I talk to my friends about what I am reading<br>• I talk to my family about what I am reading<br>• I read to find out about things I want to learn<br>• I read comic books or comics<br>• I read books that explain things<br>• I read magazines<br>• I read directions or instructions<br>• I read subtitles on the television screen |
| 'talking about reading' | • I talk to my friends about what I am reading<br>• I talk to other children about what I have read<br>• I like talking about books with other people |
| 'use of computers' | • I use a computer at home<br>• I use a computer somewhere else (not home/school)<br>• I play computer games<br>• I use the computer to write reports or stories<br>• I use the computer to look up information<br>• I send and read e-mails |
| 'TV viewing habits' | • I watch television or videos outside school<br>• Amount of time spent watching television or videos outside school on a normal school day |

**Table A2.3   School factors in multilevel analysis**

| | School questionnaire |
|---|---|
| **'attainment on entry to year 1'** | • About how many of the children in your school can do the following when they begin year 1: recognise most of the letters of the alphabet? read some words? read sentences? write letters of the alphabet? write some words? |
| **'disadvantaged background'** | • Is your school located in a town or a city? |
| | • How would you characterise the area in which your school is located? |
| | • Of children who were enrolled in your school at the start of the school year last year, about what percentage was still enrolled at the end of the school year? |
| | • Approximately what percentage of children in your school... |
| | …come from economically disadvantaged homes? |
| | …come from economically affluent homes? |
| | …were born in another country? |
| | …receive some teaching at school in their home language (other than English)? |
| | • Approximately what percentage of years 1 to 5 children in your school ... |
| | …have special needs related to reading in English? |
| | …receive extra teaching in reading due to reading difficulties in English? |
| | • Is an adult literacy programme available at your school site for the children and families in your school? |
| | • Approximately what percentage of children in your school have parents or guardians who do fundraising and other support activities for the school? |
| | • How would you characterise parental support for pupil achievement in your school? |

# References

BROOKS, G., PUGH, A.K. and SCHAGEN, I. (1996). *Reading Performance at Nine.* Slough: National Foundation for Educational Research.

CAMPBELL, J.R., KELLY, D.L., MULLIS, I.V.S., MARTIN, M.O. and SAINSBURY, M. (2001). *Framework and Specifications for PIRLS Assessment 2001.* Second edn. Chestnut Hill, MA: Boston College, PIRLS International Study Center.

DEPARTMENT FOR EDUCATION AND SKILLS (2002). *The Autumn Package 2002. Pupil Performance Information: Key Stage 2.* London: Department for Education and Skills.

ELLEY, W.B. (1992). *How in the World Do Students Read? IEA Study of Reading Literacy.* The Hague: International Association for the Evaluation of Educational Achievement.

FOY, P. and JONCAS, M. (2002). 'PIRLS sampling design.' In: MARTIN, M.O., MULLIS, I.V.S. and KENNEDY, A.M. (Eds) PIRLS Technical Report [online]. Available: http://isc.bc.edu/pirls2001i/technical.htm [25 March, 2003].

GILL, B., DUNN, M. and GODDARD, E. (2002). *Student Achievement in England: Results in Reading, Mathematical and Scientific Literacy among 15-year-olds from OECD PISA 2000 Study.* London: The Stationery Office.

GONZALEZ, E., HASTEDT, D. and KENNEDY, A. (2002). 'PIRLS survey operations procedures.' In: MARTIN, M.O., MULLIS, I.V.S. and KENNEDY, A.M. (Eds) *PIRLS Technical Report* [online]. Available: http://isc.bc.edu/pirls2001i/technical.htm [25 March, 2003].

MULLIS, I.V.S., MARTIN, M.O., GONZALEZ, E.J. and KENNEDY, A.M. (2003). *PIRLS 2001 International Report: IEA's Study of Reading Literacy Achievement in Primary School in 35 Countries.* Boston, MA: Boston College, International Study Center.

MULLIS, I.V.S., MARTIN, M.O., KENNEDY, A.M. and FLAHERTY, C.L. (Eds) (2002). *PIRLS 2001 Encyclopedia: A Reference Guide to Reading Education in the Countries Participating in IEA's Progress in International Reading Literacy Study (PIRLS).* Boston, MA: Boston College, International Study Center.

QUALIFICATIONS AND CURRICULUM AUTHORITY (2003). *Standards at Key Stage 2: English, Mathematics and Science. A Report for Headteachers, Class Teachers and Assessment Coordinators on the 2002 National Curriculum Assessment for 11-year-olds.* London: Qualifications and Curriculum Authority.

SAINSBURY, M. and CAMPBELL, J. (2002). 'Developing the PIRLS reading assessment scoring guides.' In: MARTIN, M.O., MULLIS, I.V.S. and KENNEDY, A.M. (Eds) *PIRLS Technical Report* [online]. Available: http://isc.bc.edu/pirls2001i/technical.htm [25 March, 2003].